Collins

White Rose Maths
Edexcel GCSE 9-1 Revision Guide

Aiming for Grade 5/6

Series editor: Ian Davies
Authors: Matthew Ainscough, Simon Bond, Robert Clasper, Ian Davies, Emily Fox, James Hunter, Rhys Jowett and Sahar Shillabeer

Published by Collins
An imprint of HarperCollins*Publishers*
1 London Bridge Street
London SE1 9GF

HarperCollins*Publishers*
1st Floor, Watermarque Building,
Ringsend Road, Dublin 4, Ireland

ISBN: 978-0-00-853240-6

First published 2022

10 9 8 7 6 5 4 3 2 1

British Library Cataloguing in Publication Data.

A CIP record of this book is available from the British Library.

Series editor: Ian Davies
Authors: Matthew Ainscough, Simon Bond, Robert Clasper, Ian Davies, Emily Fox, James Hunter, Rhys Jowett
and Sahar Shillabeer
Publishers: Katie Sergeant and Clare Souza
Project management and editorial: Richard Toms and Amanda Dickson
Inside concept design: Ian Wrigley
Typesetting: Nicola Lancashire (Rose and Thorn Creative Services)
Cover design: Sarah Duxbury
Production: Lyndsey Rogers
Printed in the United Kingdom by Martins the Printers

MIX
Paper from
responsible source
FSC
www.fsc.org
FSC™ C007454

This book is produced from independently certified FSC™ paper
to ensure responsible forest management.

For more information visit: www.harpercollins.co.uk/green

Contents

Introduction

How to use this revision guide

Welcome to the *Collins White Rose Maths Edexcel GCSE 9–1 Revision Guide – Aiming for Grade 5/6*. In this guide, you will revisit all the key topics you need to know and get plenty of practice to reinforce the knowledge, skills and understanding you need. The guide is suitable if you are sitting either Foundation tier aiming for a grade 5 or Higher tier with a target grade of 5 or 6.

We hope you enjoy your learning journey. Here is a short guide to how to get the most out of this book.

Inside a unit

At the start of each section, there are some basics you should already know if you are aiming for a grade 5 or 6. Key facts and practice questions are provided for each of these topics. If you are not sure about this material, you will find support in the *Collins White Rose Maths Edexcel GCSE 9–1 Revision Guide – Aiming for Grade 4* (ISBN 978-0-00-853239-0). After this, each topic is covered on a double page with everything you need to know and material for you to practise.

Facts

The 'Facts' part reminds you about what you need to know about each topic in order to succeed. This includes models and diagrams to support your understanding and definitions of key words.

Foundations

A few questions to make sure you know the basics you need to be able to do well at this topic. These are covered in detail in the *Collins White Rose Maths Edexcel GCSE 9–1 Revision Guide – Aiming for Grade 4*.

Focus

The 'Focus' part gives you worked examples on the topic you're revising. Alongside a step-by-step solution that models how you would answer exam questions, there is a detailed commentary which explains the working.

Many of the units in this guide can be tackled without a calculator, but feel free to use one to support you when you need to. Keep both your number and your calculator skills sharp by working both ways and checking your answers whenever you can.

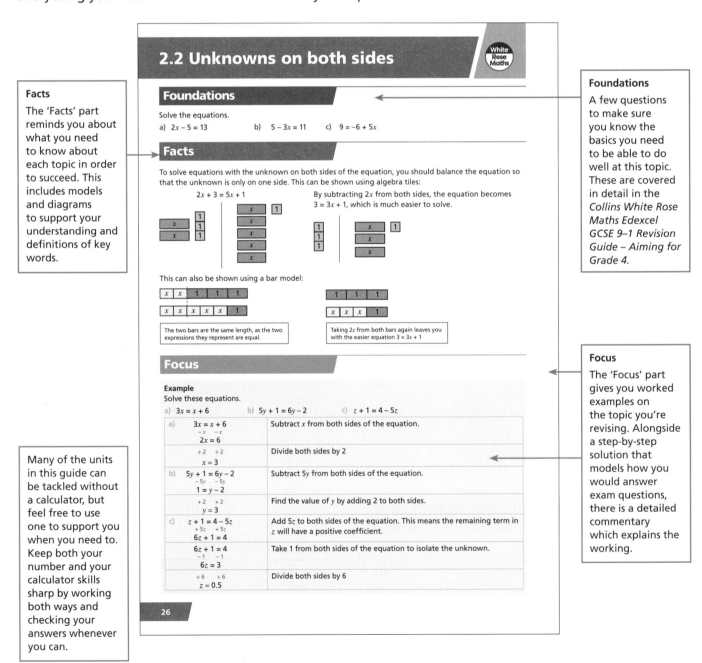

Fluency

In the 'Fluency' part, you have an opportunity to demonstrate your learning of the topic through short, targeted questions. You can check your answers at the back of the book to see how well you have done.

Fluency

1. Some coloured counters are in a bag. On 200 occasions, a counter is selected at random, its colour noted and the counter is returned to the bag. The results are shown in the table.

Outcome	Red	Yellow	Blue
Frequency	60	125	15
Relative frequency	$\frac{60}{200} = 0.3$		

Complete the table to show the relative frequency for each colour.

2. The spinner is spun 1600 times.

   a) If the spinner is fair, estimate how many times it will land on red.

   The spinner actually lands on red 608 times.

   b) Find the relative frequency of landing on red.

3. A spinner is divided into three equal sections, as shown.

   Rosie spins the spinner 120 times. The spinner lands on red 30 times, green 46 times and blue 44 times.

   a) Explain why the relative frequency of landing on red is 25%

   b) Estimate the probability that the spinner lands on blue.

   c) Is the spinner biased? Give a reason for your answer.

4. A fair spinner is split into five equal sections labelled 1 to 5. The spinner is spun 300 times.

   The relative frequency of landing on the number 4 is 0.39

   How many times did the spinner land on the number 4?

Further

1. Emily is practising netball. She throws six sets of 10 balls from the same point, and notes how many times she scores a goal. Here are her results: 8   6   7   10   6   8

   a) Complete the table.   (2 marks)

Total number of throws	10	20	30	40	50	60
Total number of goals	8	14				
Relative frequency of scoring a goal	0.8					

   b) Draw a graph to show how the relative frequency of scoring a goal changes.   (2 marks)

   c) Estimate the probability that Emily scores a goal.   (1 mark)

2. There are 20 coloured balls in a bag. One ball is chosen at random and then replaced in the bag. The results are shown in the table below.

Colour	Green	Red	Blue	Yellow
Frequency	8	29	44	19

   Estimate how many balls of each colour there are in the bag.   (3 marks)

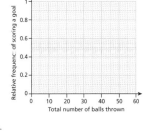

3. A biased coin is thrown x times and it lands on heads y times.

   a) Write an expression for the relative frequency of the coin landing on heads.   (2 marks)

   b) The coin is thrown 100 times.

   Write an expression for the number of times you would expect the coin to land on heads.   (1 mark)

Relative frequency   **101**

You will need separate sheets of paper, including graph paper, to complete the questions in the 'Fluency' and 'Further' parts.

Further

In the 'Further' part, you will have the chance to dive a little deeper into the topic. These questions will be a little longer and may also link to other areas of mathematics. Some of these will be examination-style questions and more detail is provided in the answers to help you see what you need to do. Some of these questions might even push you to a grade 7!

Answers to all the Practice, Foundations, Fluency and Further questions can be found from page 118.

If you are confident with everything in this guide, you should be well on your way to your target grade of 5 or 6 in GCSE mathematics. If you want to push yourself further, *Collins White Rose Maths Edexcel GCSE 9–1 Revision Guide – Aiming for Grade 7/8/9* (ISBN 978-0-00-853241-3) is also available.

Good luck with your studying and your examinations!

Ian Davies
Series Editor

Facts

When calculating with integers, always consider whether it is more appropriate to use a **mental**, **written** or **calculator** method.

For example, 1634 + 998 can be thought of as 1634 + 1000 – 2 = 2634 – 2 = 2632, rather than using a written method with a lot of exchanges where you might make a mistake.

When using the **formal written methods of addition and subtraction,** be careful to keep columns aligned and show exchanges clearly.

$$
\begin{array}{r}
5\ 8\ 6\ 2 \\
+\ 3\ 4\ 7\ 9 \\
\hline
9\ 3\ 4\ 1 \\
\end{array}
$$

$$
\begin{array}{r}
^6\!7\ ^1 6\ ^3\!4\ ^1 1 \\
-\ 3\ 8\ 2\ 7 \\
\hline
3\ 8\ 1\ 4 \\
\end{array}
$$

With decimal calculations, you may need to add in decimal points and extra zeros. For example, here is 64 – 12.67 ⟶

$$
\begin{array}{r}
6\ ^3\!4\ \cdot\!^9\!0\ ^1 0 \\
-\ 1\ 2\ \cdot\ 6\ 7 \\
\hline
5\ 1\ \cdot\ 3\ 3 \\
\end{array}
$$

You can also use a number line:

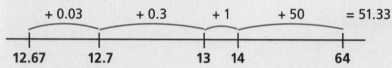

There are many different methods for multiplication; use the one with which you are most comfortable. Here are some examples:

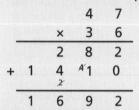
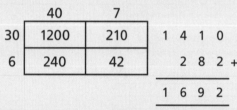
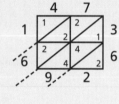

You can use your knowledge of place value to find answers to decimal calculations. For example:

47 × 36 = 1692
÷ 10 ⟨ ↓ ÷ 10 ⟩ ÷ 100
4.7 × 3.6 = 16.92

You may need to use the formal methods of short division or long division. For example:

$$
6\overline{\smash{\big)}2\ 3\ ^5 2\ ^4 2} = 3\ 8\ 7
$$

$$
17\overline{\smash{\big)}4\ 1\ 3\ 1} = 2\ 4\ 3
$$

Adding a negative number to another value will **decrease** the value of the first number. For example, 3 + –5 = –2

Subtracting a negative number from another value will **increase** the value of the first number. For example, 3 – –5 = 8

The product of a negative and a positive value is always negative.

The result of a division with one positive and one negative value is always negative.

The product of two negative numbers is always positive.

The result of dividing with two negative values is always positive.

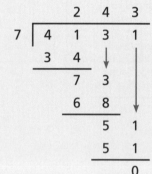

You should also know how to use your calculator efficiently. Do the Practice questions using written methods and check your answers with a calculator.

Practice

1. Work out:

   a) 784 + 98   b) 723 + 586   c) 64.7 + 38.8

   d) £18.56 + £9.99   e) £187.45 + £74.83

   > It is always useful to do an estimate before you perform the full calculation, so you know the approximate size of the correct answer.

2. Work out:

   a) 784 – 98   b) 723 – 586   c) 64.7 – 38.8

   d) £18.56 – £9.99   e) £187.45 – £74.83

3. The population of Leeds is 526 043

   The population of Bradford is 372 828

   a) How many more people live in Leeds than in Bradford?

   b) Show that the total population of Leeds and Bradford is less than 900 000

4. Work out   72.4 – 12.9 – 3.82 + 42.98

5. Work out: a) 58 × 76   b) 62.3 × 7   c) 7.4^2

6. Flo buys 8 pencils for 78p each.

   She pays with a £20 note.

   How much change should Flo receive?

7. Faith works 37 hours one week.

   She is paid £8.45 per hour.

   Work out Faith's wage for the week.

8. Work out: a) 113.2 ÷ 4   b) 1288 ÷ 23

9. A rugby club hires coaches to transport 870 fans to an away match.

   Each coach holds 52 people.

   a) How many coaches are needed?

   b) How many seats are left over?

10. Marta buys a car.

    The total cost of the car is £14 000

    She pays a deposit of £3500 and the rest in 12 equal monthly payments.

    How much is each monthly payment?

11. Work out: a) –5 + 3   b) –5 – 3   c) –5 + –3   d) –5 – –3

12. Work out: a) –5 × –3   b) 5 × –3   c) –15 ÷ 3   d) 30 ÷ –5   e) $(–5)^2$

Facts

Equivalent fractions have the same value and can be found by multiplying or dividing the numerator and denominator of the fraction by the same number.

Writing fractions as tenths, hundredths, thousandths, etc. helps to **convert them to decimals**.

$$\frac{3}{5} = \frac{6}{10} = 0.6 \qquad \frac{143}{200} = \frac{715}{1000} = 0.715$$

You can also use **division**.

$$\frac{3}{8} = 3 \div 8 \qquad 8 \overline{)3 \cdot {}^3 0 \; {}^6 0 \; {}^4 0}$$

$$\begin{array}{c} 0 \cdot 3 \; 7 \; 5 \end{array}$$

You can also convert decimals to fractions.

$$0.475 = \frac{475}{1000} = \frac{95}{200} = \frac{19}{40}$$

A fraction is **improper** if the numerator is greater than the denominator, such as $\frac{11}{7}$, and it can be converted to a **mixed number**, in this case $1\frac{4}{7}$. Diagrams can help to visualise this:

$$\frac{11}{7} = 1\frac{4}{7}$$

To **add or subtract fractions with the same denominator**, you add or subtract the numerators.

$$\frac{8}{11} - \frac{3}{11} = \frac{5}{11} \qquad \frac{6}{7} + \frac{5}{7} = \frac{11}{7} = 1\frac{4}{7}$$

When the denominators are different, first use **equivalent fractions** to find a common denominator:

$$\frac{7}{12} - \frac{4}{9} = \frac{21}{36} - \frac{16}{36} = \frac{5}{36}$$

When adding or subtracting mixed numbers, you can deal with the wholes and fractional parts separately or convert to improper fractions as appropriate. For example:

$$8\frac{3}{5} + 6\frac{5}{8} = 8 + 6 + \frac{3}{5} + \frac{5}{8} = 14 + \frac{24}{40} + \frac{25}{40} = 14\frac{49}{40} = 15\frac{9}{40}$$

To **multiply** fractions, you multiply the numerators and the denominators together: $\frac{3}{5} \times \frac{4}{7} = \frac{12}{35}$

Look for factors to make the calculations easier: $\frac{7^1}{12_4} \times \frac{9^3}{14_2} = \frac{3}{8}$

The **reciprocal** of a fraction is found by swapping the numerator and denominator. For example, the reciprocal of $\frac{3}{5}$ is $\frac{5}{3}$. Notice that the product of a fraction and its reciprocal is always 1

$$\frac{3}{5} \times \frac{5}{3} = \frac{15}{15} = 1$$

To **divide by a fraction**, you multiply by its reciprocal.

$$\frac{3}{5} \div \frac{2}{9} = \frac{3}{5} \times \frac{9}{2} = \frac{27}{10} = 2\frac{7}{10}$$

When multiplying or dividing mixed numbers, always write them as improper fractions first.

$$2\frac{2}{3} \div 1\frac{1}{5} = \frac{8}{3} \div \frac{6}{5} = \frac{8}{3} \times \frac{5}{6} = \frac{40}{18} = \frac{20}{9} = 2\frac{2}{9}$$

Bar models are very useful when working with fractions of an amount.

Find $\frac{2}{5}$ of 40

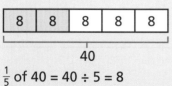

$$\frac{1}{5} \text{ of } 40 = 40 \div 5 = 8$$

So $\frac{2}{5}$ of $40 = 2 \times 8 = 16$

$\frac{2}{5}$ of $x = 40$. Find x.

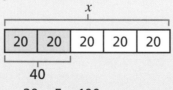

$$x = 20 \times 5 = 100$$

You should also know how to use the fraction button on your calculator. Do the Practice questions using written methods and check your answers with a calculator.

Practice

1. Write the fractions in simplest form.

   a) $\frac{180}{300}$ b) $\frac{248}{600}$ c) $\frac{275}{500}$

2. Write the fractions as decimals.

   a) $\frac{11}{50}$ b) $\frac{109}{200}$ c) $\frac{81}{250}$ d) $\frac{17}{20}$ e) $\frac{17}{40}$ f) $\frac{5}{8}$

3. Convert the decimals to fractions in simplest form.

   a) 0.65   b) 0.624   c) 0.275   d) 0.356

4. Which is greater, $\frac{18}{5}$ or $3\frac{3}{4}$?

   Explain your answer.

5. Work out the answers to these calculations, giving your answers in their simplest form.

   a) $\frac{3}{4} + \frac{1}{6}$ b) $\frac{3}{4} \times \frac{1}{6}$ c) $\frac{3}{4} - \frac{1}{6}$ d) $\frac{3}{4} \div \frac{1}{6}$

6. Work out:

   a) $5\frac{2}{3} - 2\frac{1}{4}$ b) $3\frac{5}{8} + 7\frac{5}{6}$ c) $6\frac{2}{3} \times 2\frac{1}{5}$

   d) $6\frac{2}{3} \div 2$ e) $6\frac{2}{3} \div \frac{1}{2}$ f) $6\frac{2}{3} \div 2\frac{1}{2}$

7. Work out the area of the triangle.

$$3\frac{5}{6} \times 1\frac{3}{8} = \frac{23}{6} \times \frac{11}{8} = \frac{253}{48}$$

$$\frac{253}{48} \times \frac{1}{2} = \frac{253}{96} = 3\frac{35}{96}$$

$3\frac{5}{6}$ m

$1\frac{3}{8}$ m

8. The triangle and the rectangle have the same area:

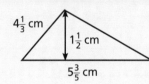

$4\frac{1}{3}$ cm

$1\frac{1}{2}$ cm

$5\frac{3}{5}$ cm

$4\frac{3}{4}$ cm

   Find the width of the rectangle.

9. Work out: a) $\frac{3}{7}$ of 84   b) $\frac{11}{3}$ of 60

10. $\frac{5}{6}$ of a number is 400

    Work out $\frac{3}{5}$ of the number.

Facts

A **percentage** such as 45% (read as 'forty-five percent') is a number of parts per hundred. A percentage can be represented as a fraction ($\frac{45}{100}$ which simplifies to $\frac{9}{20}$) or as a decimal (0.45, the result of 45 ÷ 100). You should know these key equivalences:

Percentage	Fraction	Decimal
50%	$\frac{1}{2}$	0.5
25%	$\frac{1}{4}$	0.25
10%	$\frac{1}{10}$	0.1
$33\frac{1}{3}$%	$\frac{1}{3}$	0.333... = 0.$\dot{3}$

You can also use multiples of these facts. For example:

$70\% = 7 \times 10\% = \frac{7}{10} = 0.7$

$75\% = 3 \times 25\% = \frac{3}{4} = 0.75$

$66\frac{2}{3}\% = 2 \times 33\frac{1}{3}\% = \frac{2}{3} = 0.\dot{6}$

There are many ways to **calculate percentages of amounts**.

For example, to find 45% of 60 you could:

- find 50% (60 ÷ 2 = 30), find 5% (50% ÷ 10 = 30 ÷ 10 = 3) and subtract (45% = 50% − 5% = 30 − 3 = 27)
- find 1% (60 ÷ 100) and multiply the answer by 45
- use the fraction multiplication $\frac{45}{100} \times 60$
- use a **decimal multiplier** by working out 0.45 × 60; this is the most efficient way if you have a calculator, especially when working with more challenging percentages such as 37% or 1.6%

To **express one amount as a percentage of another**, you can:

- express as a fraction and convert. For example, a mark of 24 out of 60 as a percentage is $\frac{24}{60} = \frac{2}{5} = \frac{4}{10} = 40\%$
- divide and convert the decimal, if you have a calculator. For example, if 6 out of 32 students are absent, then 6 ÷ 32 = 0.1875 = 18.75% ≈ 19% are absent.

Bar models are very useful to represent **percentage changes**, with the original value being represented by 100%

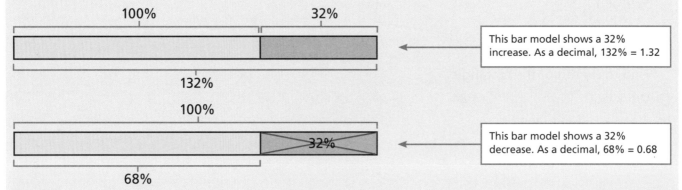

A quick way to increase or decrease a number by a percentage is to use a multiplier.

If you **increase** an amount by 32%, you now have 132% of the original, so you can multiply by 1.32

If you **decrease** an amount by 32%, you now have 68% of the original, so you can multiply by 0.68

Practice

1 Complete the table of equivalences, writing fractions in their simplest form.

Percentage	Fraction	Decimal
40%		0.4
60%		0.6
6%		0.06
5%		0.05
	$\frac{7}{20}$	

2 Without using a calculator, work out:

a) 25% of 80 kg b) 30% of 200 g c) 90% of 60 m

d) 75% of £3000 e) 120% of 70 cm f) 350% of £600

3 Find at least three different ways to calculate 45% of £90

4 Use a calculator to work out:

a) 73% of 90 kg b) 31% of £750 c) 17% of 600 ml d) 28% of £9000

e) 9.6% of £4000 f) 1.2% of 30 kg g) 128.7% of £800 h) 210.67% of 8 km

5 Which is greater, 60% of £300 or 35% of £500?

6 Write $\frac{2}{3}$ as a percentage.

7 A firm employs 80 people.

Thirty-eight of the people are less than 30 years old.

What percentage of the people who work for the firm are less than 30 years old?

8 Explain why 80% of 60 = 60% of 80

9 Write these numbers in order of size, starting with the smallest:

35% $\frac{1}{3}$ 30.5%   0.299 $\frac{2}{5}$

10 Jackson says that 23% is greater than 0.4

Explain why Jackson is wrong.

11 Which is greater, 35% of 102 or 36% of 97? Justify your answer.

12 Huda buys a tablet for £600

She pays a deposit of 35% and the rest in 12 equal payments.

How much is each payment?

13 Faith invests £600 in a bank account. The bank account pays simple interest at a rate of 3.5% per year.

Work out the total amount of interest Faith earns over 3 years.

14 Zach buys a house for £280 000

He sells the house for £378 000

Calculate the percentage profit Zach makes.

15 Abdullah earns £36 000 a year.

He gets a 1.5% pay rise.

Calculate his monthly wage after the pay rise.

Foundations

1 Find:
    a) 80% of £64
    b) 140% of £60

2 Solve these equations.
    a) $0.7x = 35$
    b) $1.2x = 72.6$

Facts

Per cent means parts per hundred. The **original value** is the amount before a change takes place.

In **reverse percentage** questions, you need to find the original value.

When a value has been increased by 15%, the new value is 115% of the original value:

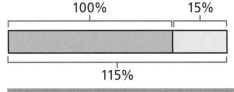

When a value has been decreased by 15%, the new value is 85% of the original value:

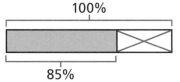

Focus

Example 1

The price of a chair is reduced by 30% to £210

What was the price of the chair before the reduction?

100% − 30% = 70% ![bar model]	Work out what percentage of the original price is left after the reduction.
$\div 7 \left(\begin{array}{l} 70\% = £210 \\ 10\% = £30 \\ 100\% = £300 \end{array} \right) \div 7$ $\times 10$ $\times 10$ Original price of the chair was £300	70% of the original price is £210, so 10% of the original price is £210 ÷ 7 = £30 The original price is 100%, which is 10 × 10% or 10 × £30 = £300

Alternative method

100% − 30% = 70% 70% = 0.7	As before, work out what percentage of the original price is left after the reduction.
Let £x be the original price before the reduction. £$x \times 0.7 = £210$	Set up an equation to show the change.
$x = £210 \div 0.7 = £300$	Solve the equation to find the original price.

Example 2

After a 4% pay rise, James earns £33 280 a year. What was his salary before the increase?

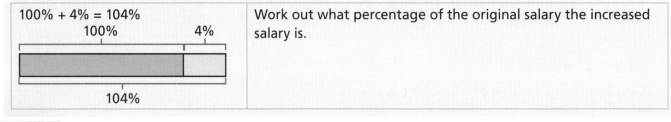

100% + 4% = 104% ![bar model]	Work out what percentage of the original salary the increased salary is.

$\div 104 \left(\begin{array}{l} 104\% = \text{£}33\,280 \\ 1\% = \text{£}320 \\ 100\% = \text{£}32\,000 \end{array} \right) \div 104$
$\times 100 \qquad\qquad\qquad\quad \times 100$

| You know 104% |
| Find 1% by dividing by 104 |
| Find the original (100%) by multiplying 1% by 100 |

Alternatively, you could solve the equation $1.04x = 33\,280$

Fluency

1 60% of a number is 54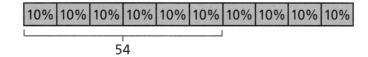

54

Work out:

a) 10% of the number   b) 5% of the number   c) 40% of the number   d) 100% of the number

2 40% of the students in a class are boys. There are 14 boys in the class.

How many students are in the class?

3 In a sale, a shop reduces the price of all its books by 15%. The price of a book is now £5.95

Work out the original cost of the book.

4 A special-offer box of tea bags contains 35% more than a normal box. The special-offer box contains 1080 tea bags.

How many tea bags are in a normal box?

5 Lola scores 68 marks on a test. Lola's teacher tells her that this is 85% of the marks.

What is the maximum score on the test?

6 The price of a laptop is £330, including VAT at 20%

Work out the price of the laptop before VAT was added.

7 The value of an investment drops by 7% to £34 804.26

What was the value of the investment before the drop?

8 A savings account pays 4.5% interest per annum. Millie invests some money into the savings account, and at the end of the first year she has £5068.25 in the account.

How much money did she make in interest in the year?

Further

1 A school opens a new sixth-form centre and increases the number of students to 1640. A teacher says this is exactly 40% more students than previously.

Explain why the teacher cannot be correct.   (2 marks)

2 65% of 270 = 15% of A

Find the value of A.   (2 marks)

3 A square is enlarged so that the area increases by 25%

The area of the enlarged square is 100 cm²

Calculate the side length of the original square, giving your answer to 1 decimal place.   (2 marks)

4 In a sale, a shop reduces the price of all items by 20%. A week later, prices are reduced by a further 15%. A pair of jeans now cost £44.19

a) Explain why the price has not been reduced by 35% altogether.   (1 mark)

b) Find the cost of the jeans before the sale began.   (2 marks)

1.2 Exact answers

Foundations

1 Write down the radius and the diameter of each circle.

 9 mm

 3.4 m

2 Solve the equation $5 + 3p = 10$, giving your answer as an improper fraction.

Facts

Giving an answer as an **exact value** means that you should not use decimal form. For example, you could give your answer as a fraction, a multiple of π (the ratio of the circumference of a circle to its diameter) or as a **surd** (a root that cannot be written as an integer).

Examples of exact answers include: $\frac{7}{5}$ $1\frac{2}{5}$ 10π $\sqrt{7}$ $\frac{\sqrt{3}}{2}$

When looking at multiples of π, for example $5\frac{1}{2}\pi$ or 5.5π, it is better to write $\frac{11}{2}\pi$

Focus

Example 1

a) Calculate the circumference of the circle, giving your answer in terms of π

b) Calculate the area of the circle, giving your answer in terms of π

 3 cm

a) Circumference $= \pi \times d$ $= \pi \times 3$ $= 3\pi$ cm	The circumference of a circle is given by the formula circumference $= \pi \times$ diameter
	When writing your answer in terms of π, you should always write the number before the symbol. Make sure you include the units with your answer.
b) Area $= \pi r^2$ $r = \frac{3}{2}$ cm $\text{Area} = \pi \times \left(\frac{3}{2}\right)^2$ $\text{Area} = \frac{9}{4}\pi$ cm^2	Start with the formula for the area of a circle.
	You are given the diameter, so first you need to find the radius, by dividing by 2
	When you square a number, you multiply it by itself so $\left(\frac{3}{2}\right)^2 = \frac{3}{2} \times \frac{3}{2}$

Example 2

a) Show that the exact value of YZ is $\sqrt{3}$ cm.

b) Use the diagram to write down the exact value of tan 30°

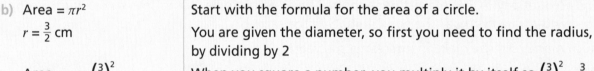

a) 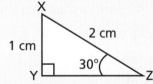	The triangle is right-angled, so you can use Pythagoras' theorem to find the missing length. Label the sides of the triangle a, b, and c where c is the hypotenuse. It doesn't matter which is a and which is b.
$a^2 + b^2 = c^2$	Use Pythagoras' theorem.
$1^2 + b^2 = c^2$ $1 + b^2 = 4$	Substitute the values you know into the formula and solve for b.

$b^2 = 3$ $b = \sqrt{3}$ The exact value of YZ is $\sqrt{3}$ cm.	This is exact, but 1.7320... would be an approximation.
b) 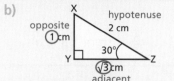	Label the triangle sides as opposite, adjacent and hypotenuse. See units 4.11 and 4.12 for more about using trigonometry in right-angled triangles.
$\tan \theta = \frac{\text{opposite}}{\text{adjacent}}$ $\tan 30° = \frac{1}{\sqrt{3}}$	Use the formula for the tangent ratio and substitute in the values you know. If you check on a calculator, it may give the answer in a different form as $\frac{\sqrt{3}}{3}$, which is equivalent.

Fluency

1 Solve the equations, giving your answers as fractions.

a) $7 + 2g = 10$ b) $5h - 4 = 4$ c) $9 = 9c - 8$ d) $6 - 4b = 1$

2 a) Calculate the circumference of the circle, giving your answer in terms of π

    b) Calculate the area of the circle, giving your answer in terms of π

3 Here is a right-angled triangle:

Work out the exact value of EG.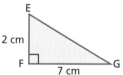

4 Solve the equations, giving your answers as surds.

a) $2x^2 = 22$ b) $7 + 2w^2 = 27$

5 Find the volumes of the shapes, giving your answers in terms of π

a) 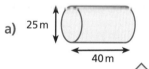   b)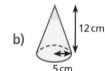

See unit 4.7 for information about calculating volume.

6 A large square has a side length of 6 cm.

A small square joins the midpoints of the larger square.

Calculate the exact length of a side of the small square.

7 Use the diagram to write down the exact values of:

a) $\cos 45°$ b) $\tan 45°$

Further

1 Calculate the perimeter of the shape, giving your answer in terms of π (3 marks)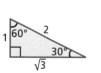

15 cm

2 Use the diagrams to find the exact values of the expressions.

a) $\sin 45°$ (1 mark)   b) $\cos 30°$ (1 mark)

c) $\sin 60°$ (1 mark)   d) $\tan 60°$ (1 mark)

These ratios are covered in detail in unit 4.13

3 A cone has a radius of 9 cm and a volume of 850 cm³

Calculate the height of the cone, giving your answer in terms of π (3 marks)   Use the formula $V = \frac{1}{3}\pi r^2 h$

4 Calculate the exact values of x and y. (4 marks)

Exact answers   **15**

1.3 Limits of accuracy

Foundations

Round 728.561 to:

a) 1 decimal place   b) the nearest integer   c) the nearest ten   d) 1 significant figure

Facts

Limits of accuracy tell you the greatest and the least numbers that a rounded answer could actually be. For example, if a length is 140 cm measured to the nearest 10 cm, the actual length could be anything from 135 cm up to (but not including) 145 cm.

This can be shown as an **error interval** using inequality symbols as $135 \leqslant l < 145$, where l is the length in cm, or shown on a number line:

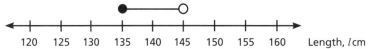

Remember that when you **truncate** a number, you remove numbers rather than rounding to the nearest integer, tenth, etc. For example, 32.87 truncated to 1 decimal place is 32.8

Focus

Example 1
The length of a swimming pool is 50 metres, correct to the nearest metre.

a) What is the shortest possible length of the pool?   b) Write the error interval for the length, l, of the pool.

a) 49.5 m	This is the first number that will round to 50 to the nearest whole number, for example 49.47 will round to 49
b) $49.5 \leqslant l < 50.5$	Notice that 49.5 is included in the error interval as 49.5 rounds to 50 to the nearest metre.
	50.5 would round to 51 to the nearest metre, so 50.5 is not included in the error interval.
	You read the error interval as 'l is greater than or equal to 49.5 and less than 50.5'

Example 2
The price of a house is £150 000

a) Write the error interval for the price, p, if the price has been rounded to 2 significant figures.
b) Write the error interval for the price, p, if the price has been truncated to 2 significant figures.

a) £145 000 $\leqslant p <$ £155 000	Notice that £145 000 is included in the error interval as £145 000 rounds to £150 000 to the nearest ten thousand.
	£155 000 would round to £160 000 to the nearest ten thousand, so it is not included in the error interval.
b) £150 000 $\leqslant p <$ £160 000	Remember that when you truncate a number, you remove numbers rather than rounding them.
	The smallest value of the thousands digit has to be 0 so that the number truncates to £150 000
	£160 000 would truncate to £160 000 to the nearest ten thousand, so it is not included in the error interval.

Fluency

1 Here are some numbers:

7.7   6.64   7.54   6.57   7.706   7.05   6.599

Which of these numbers round to:

a) 7 to the nearest integer?   b) 6.6 to 1 decimal place?   c) 8 to 1 significant figure?

2 $y = 7$ to the nearest integer.

Which is the correct error interval for y?

$6.5 < y < 7.5$ $6.5 < y \leqslant 7.5$ $6.5 \leqslant y < 7.5$ $6.5 \leqslant y \leqslant 7.5$

3 A number, x, is 300 when rounded to 1 significant figure.

Complete the error interval for x. .... $\leqslant x <$ ....

You may use the number line to help you.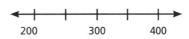

4 The distance, d miles, between two towns is given by the error interval $72.5 \leqslant d < 73.5$

a) Write down two possible values of d correct to 1 decimal place.

b) What is the value of d correct to the nearest integer?

5 The number of people who attended a tennis match is 40 000, rounded to the nearest thousand.

a) What is the smallest number of people who could have been at the tennis match?

b) What is the greatest number of people who could have been at the tennis match?

c) Write the error interval for the number of people, n, who attended the tennis match.

6 a) Which of these numbers are equal to 75 000 when truncated to 2 significant figures?

75 650   74 800   75 900   75 050   7 510 000

b) A number, x, when truncated to the nearest integer, is 15

Write an error interval for x.

7 A number, n, when rounded, is 100

Write the error interval for n if it has been rounded to:

a) 1 significant figure   b) 2 significant figures   c) 3 significant figures

Further

1 A number, n, is 600 when rounded to 1 significant figure.

What is the same and what is different about the possible values of n if it represents the number of people in a theatre, or it represents a length?   (2 marks)

2 Write a possible description for each error interval.

a) $70.05 \leqslant g < 70.15$ (1 mark)   b) $7905 \leqslant h < 7915$ (1 mark)   c) $79\,995 \leqslant k < 80\,005$ (1 mark)

3 The length of a regular pentagon is given as 8 cm, correct to the nearest centimetre.

a) Write the error interval for the length, l, of the pentagon.   (2 marks)

b) Write the error interval for the perimeter, p, of the pentagon.   (2 marks)

4 $x = 3.6$ and $y = 8.1$, both correct to the nearest tenth.

a) Find the error interval for the expression $x + y$ (2 marks)

b) Find the error interval for the expression $y - x$ (2 marks)

Limits of accuracy   17

1.4 Calculator and non-calculator methods

Foundations

1 Work out:

a) $5 + -3$ b) $-5 + -3$ c) $-5 - 3$ d) $-5 + 3$ e) $-5 - -3$

2 Write these numbers as ordinary numbers.   a) 3.6×10^5 b) 7.04×10^{-3}

Facts

Directed numbers

Adding a negative number is the same as a subtraction, for example $6 + -2 = 6 - 2 = 4$

Subtracting a negative number is the same as an addition, for example $9 - -2 = 9 + 2 = 11$

> See unit 1F1

The product, or quotient, of two negative numbers is a positive number, for example $-5 \times -3 = 15$

To perform calculations with directed numbers on a calculator, you will need to know how to use the sign change key, like (−) or ±

Standard form

When multiplying numbers in standard form, you can add the powers of 10 and when dividing you can subtract them.

When adding or subtracting two numbers in standard form, it is usually easier to write them as ordinary numbers.

Buttons like ×10ˣ or EXP can be used to input numbers in standard form on a calculator.

You may also need to use the fraction key like this to work with calculations.

Focus

Example 1

Evaluate $\frac{a^2 + b}{c}$ when $a = -3$, $b = 5$ and $c = -2$

$a^2 + b$ $= (-3)^2 + 5$ $= 9 + 5$ $= 14$	First you need to use substitution to work out the numerator of the fraction.
	When you square the value of negative 3, you get positive 9 (as the product of two negative numbers is positive).
	Add 9 and the value of b, 5, to get 14
$\frac{a^2 + b}{c}$ $= \frac{14}{-2}$ $= -7$	Now you know the numerator is 14, you can divide by −2
	When dividing a positive number by a negative number, the solution will always be negative.
	Therefore the solution is −7

On your calculator you can enter it like this by using the fraction button.

Example 2

Work out the calculations, giving your answers in standard form.

a) $(1.2 \times 10^3) \times (6 \times 10^5)$ b) $(1.2 \times 10^3) + (6 \times 10^5)$

a) $(1.2 \times 10^3) \times (6 \times 10^5) = 1.2 \times 6 \times 10^3 \times 10^5$ $\quad = 7.2 \times 10^{3+5}$ $\quad = 7.2 \times 10^8$	You can multiply 1.2 and 6 together first. You can then multiply 10^3 and 10^5 together. Recall that you can add the indices when you are multiplying powers of the same number. See more about index laws in unit 2.3
b) $1.2 \times 10^3 = 1.2 \times 1000 = 1200$ $6 \times 10^5 = 6 \times 100\,000 = 600\,000$ $1200 + 600\,000 = 601\,200$ $601\,200 = 6.012 \times 100\,000 = 6.012 \times 10^5$	You can begin by converting the numbers from standard form to ordinary numbers. You can then add 1200 and 600 000 together. Finish the question by writing your answer in standard form.

On your calculator, enter the standard form numbers using the $\times 10^x$ or EXP buttons and use the operation keys as usual. Check that you get the same answers as given above.

Fluency

1 Work out:

a) -5×-3 b) 5×-3 c) $-15 \div 3$ d) $30 \div -5$

2 Evaluate $\frac{2a-b}{c^2}$ when:

a) $a = 10$, $b = 4$ and $c = -2$ b) $a = 13.5$, $b = 0$ and $c = -3$ c) $a = -10$, $b = 4$ and $c = 4$

3 Work out the answers to these calculations, giving your answers in standard form. Check your answers using a calculator.

a) $(1.5 \times 10^6) + (4 \times 10^5)$ b) $(2.5 \times 10^{-3}) - (3 \times 10^{-5})$ c) $(7 \times 10^{-3}) \times (1.5 \times 10^2)$ d) $(6.4 \times 10^7) \div (2 \times 10^3)$

4 $x = 7 \times 10^3$, $y = 5 \times 10^2$ and $z = 4 \times 10^5$

Find the value of each expression, giving your answers in standard form.

a) xy b) x^2 c) $\frac{y}{z}$ d) $z - y$

5 Here are some number cards:

 4   5   10   2   −1   −2   −20   −4

Using the cards above, find at least two different ways to make each of the statements correct.

a) .... × .... = −20   b) .... ÷ .... = −5   c) −2 < .... ÷ .... < 2

Further

1 Are -5^2 and $(-5)^2$ the same or different?

Explain your answer. (2 marks)

2 The product of two numbers, A and B, is −24

The sum of A and B is −5 where $A > B$

What are the two numbers? (2 marks)

3 The distance between the Earth and the Sun is 150 million kilometres.

The speed of light is 3×10^5 km/s

Calculate the time, in seconds, it takes for light to travel from the Earth to the Sun. Give your answer in standard form. (3 marks)

Facts

Algebra is using letters to represent numbers.

Expressions such as $p - 2q$ and $x^2 + 2x + 3$ are made up of individual **terms** like p, $2q$, x^2, $2x$ and 3

When writing terms algebraically, multiplication signs are not used. So, for example, $5x$ is the simplest way of writing $5 \times x$ or $x \times 5$

$p \times p$ is written as p^2 (p **squared**) and $p \times p \times p$ is written as p^3 (p **cubed**), etc.

Divisions are written as fractions. For example, $c \div 5$ is written $\frac{c}{5}$

You can **substitute** into an expression to work out its value.

For example, when $a = 3$, $2a^2 + \frac{6}{a} = 2 \times 3^2 + \frac{6}{3} = 18 + 2 = 20$

and when $a = -2$, $2a^2 + \frac{6}{a} = 2 \times (-2)^2 + \frac{6}{-2} = 8 + -3 = 5$

Like terms can be **simplified** by adding and subtracting the **coefficients** of the terms.

For example, $8a + 6a = 14a$ (adding the coefficients 8 and 6 gives 14).

$6p + 7p^2$ cannot be simplified because the terms are **unlike**. p and p^2 are not 'like' terms.

Equations show expressions or terms that are of equal value. You can solve equations to work out values of letters. | See units 2F2 and 2.2 for more details. |

Brackets can be used to collect terms together. For example, $3(x + 5)$ is used to denote '3 lots of the expression $x + 5$'.

You **expand** brackets by multiplying every term inside the brackets by the term outside.

For example, $5(2a + 3 - b) \equiv 10a + 15 - 5b$

| The $\equiv$ sign means 'is identically equal to'. The expressions either side of the sign are true for all values of a and b. |

The reverse of expanding brackets is **factorising**. For example, $12a - 9b \equiv 3(4a - 3b)$ as 3 is a factor of both $12a$ and $9b$. When factorising, always look for the highest common factor which can be a number, a letter or a more complex term.

Statements like $3(x + 7) \equiv 3x + 21$ are called **identities**.

Sometimes letters can take different values at different times and are called **variables**. When there is a relationship between two variables, it can be expressed as an equation; for example $y = 2x + 1$, which can be shown on a **graph** by first completing a table of values to find coordinate pairs (x, y).

x	−2	0	2
$y = 2x + 1$	−3	1	5

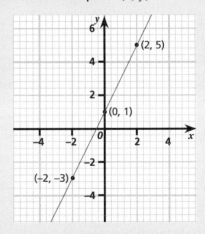

| See units 2.6 and 2.7 for more details about equations of straight lines. |

Variables can also be connected by a **formula**, which you can use to work out one value when given others. For example, $P = 2(l + w)$ is a formula for the perimeter, P, of a rectangle with length l and width w.

Practice

1. Write each of these as a single term.

   a) $7 \times p$ b) $q \times 6$ c) $c \div 9$ d) $5 \times t \times t$

   e) $6 \times k \times 7$ f) $3 \times m \times 5 \times n$ g) $5p \times 6p$ h) $10 \div m$

2. Simplify the expressions.

   a) $3p + 4q + 5p + 6q$

   b) $3p + 4q - 5p - 6q$

   c) $3p - 4q - 5p + 6q$

3. $a = 4$, $b = 6$ and $c = 9$

   Work out the value of:

   a) $a + 3b$ b) $2b^2$ c) $(2b)^2$

   d) $\frac{c}{b}$ e) $\frac{bc}{a}$ f) $10 - a(2b - c)$

4. Expand the brackets.

   a) $3(2x + y)$ b) $x(2x + y)$

   c) $3x(2x - y)$ d) $3x(10y - 5x)$

5. Expand and simplify:

   a) $3(m + 2n) + 6(n + 5m)$ b) $5(m - n) - 2(n - 3m)$

6. a) Factorise: i) $8p - 12q$ ii) $xy + 3yz - 9y$

   b) Factorise fully: i) $12ab - 18bc$ ii) $10x^2 - 5x$

7. Show that $8(2p + 4) \equiv 16(2 + p)$

8. a) Complete a table of values for $y = 3x - 4$

x	−1	0	1	2	3
y					

   b) Draw the graph of $y = 3x - 4$ for values of x from −1 to 3

9. Use the formula $p = 6t - q$ to work out:

   a) p when $t = 7$ and $q = 9$

   b) t when $p = 7$ and $q = 5$

   c) q when $p = 15$ and $t = 4$

10. Work out the values of a and b in the identity $3(x + 2y) + ax \equiv b(5x + 3y)$

2F2 Basic equations and inequalities

Facts

Equations can be solved using inverse operations and 'balancing' both sides.

$$-8 \left(\begin{array}{c} 5a + 8 = 25 \end{array} \right) -8$$

$$5a = 17$$

$$\div 5 \left(\begin{array}{c} \end{array} \right) \div 5$$

$$a = 3.4$$

$$+9 \left(\begin{array}{c} \frac{b}{4} - 9 = 70 \end{array} \right) +9$$

$$\frac{b}{4} = 79$$

$$\times 4 \left(\begin{array}{c} \end{array} \right) \times 4$$

$$b = 316$$

You can also use bar models to illustrate solving equations.

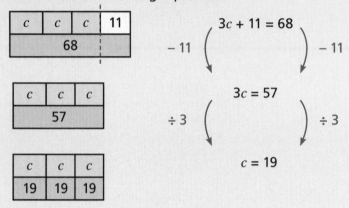

$$3c + 11 = 68$$

$$-11 \left(\right) -11$$

$$3c = 57$$

$$\div 3 \left(\right) \div 3$$

$$c = 19$$

Inequalities can be approached in the same way.

$$-8 \left(\frac{d}{7} + 8 > 2 \right) -8$$

$$\frac{d}{7} > -6$$

$$\times 7 \left(\right) \times 7$$

$$d > -42$$

$$+8 \left(15 \leqslant 4m - 8 \right) +8$$

$$23 \leqslant 4m$$

$$\div 4 \left(\right) \div 4$$

$$5.75 \leqslant m$$

If the unknown has a negative coefficient, deal with this term first to make it easier to solve.

$$+4m \left(12 - 4m = 7 \right) +4m$$

$$-7 \left(12 = 7 + 4m \right) -7$$

$$\div 4 \left(5 = 4m \right) \div 4$$

$$1.25 = m$$

$$+\frac{p}{3} \left(8 \geqslant 4 - \frac{p}{3} \right) +\frac{p}{3}$$

$$-8 \left(8 + \frac{p}{3} \geqslant 4 \right) -8$$

$$\times 3 \left(\frac{p}{3} \geqslant -4 \right) \times 3$$

$$p \geqslant -12$$

If you multiply or divide both sides of an inequality by a negative number, the direction of the inequality is reversed.

$$\div -2 \left(\begin{array}{c} -2t > 12 \end{array} \right) \div -2$$

$$t < -6$$

You can solve equations with brackets by expanding the brackets first, but you do not have to.

$$6(x + 2) = 15 \qquad \textbf{OR}$$

$$-12 \left(6x + 12 = 15 \right) -12$$

$$\div 6 \left(6x = 3 \right) \div 6$$

$$x = 0.5$$

$$\div 6 \left(6(x + 2) = 15 \right) \div 6$$

$$-2 \left(x + 2 = 2.5 \right) -2$$

$$x = 0.5$$

Practice

1. Solve the equations.

   a) $4x + 5 = 30$ b) $4x - 5 = 30$ c) $4(x + 5) = 30$ d) $4(x - 5) = 30$

   e) $\frac{x}{4} + 5 = 30$ f) $\frac{x+4}{5} = 30$ g) $\frac{x-4}{5} = 30$ h) $\frac{x}{4} - 5 = 30$

2. Solve the inequalities.

   a) $4x + 5 > 30$ b) $4x - 5 < 30$ c) $4(x + 5) \geqslant 30$ d) $4(x - 5) < 30$

   e) $\frac{x}{4} + 5 \geqslant 30$ f) $\frac{x+4}{5} < 30$ g) $\frac{x-4}{5} \geqslant 30$ h) $\frac{x}{4} - 5 < 30$

3. Ed thinks of a number.

   5 less than one-third of Ed's number is 17

   Work out Ed's number.

4. Flo thinks of a number.

   12 more than twice Flo's number is greater than 40

   Find the smallest integer value Flo's number could be.

5. Solve the equations.

   a) $12 + 4a = 20$ b) $12 - 4a = 20$

6. Solve the inequalities.

   a) $\frac{y}{4} - 6 > 10$ b) $6 + \frac{y}{4} > 10$ c) $6 - \frac{y}{4} > 10$

7. Solve the equation $p + 2p + p = 50$

8. Solve $48 = 8(t - 3)$

9. Solve $\frac{2x}{3} = 18$

10. $3x > x + 6$

    Find the smallest integer value of x.

11. $9 < 30 - 5y$

    Find the greatest integer value of y.

12. The angles in a triangle are $(2x - 10)°$, $(4x - 5)°$ and $(2x + 15)°$

    Find the size of the smallest angle in the triangle.

13. A right-angled triangle has base $3x$ cm and perpendicular height $5x$ cm.

    The area of the triangle is 480 cm²

    Work out the value of x.

2.1 Changing the subject

Foundations

Solve the equations.

a) $5x = 18$

b) $\frac{x}{5} = 18$

c) $\frac{5}{x} = 18$

d) $5 - x = 18$

e) $x + 5 = 18$

f) $5x + 3 = 18$

g) $3 - 5x = 18$

h) $\frac{5 - x}{3} = 18$

i) $\frac{x}{3} + 5 = 18$

Facts

The **subject** of a formula is the variable that is being evaluated. For example, in the formula $T = 3a - b$, T is the subject of the formula, and it is written **in terms of** a and b.

For some formulae, you can visualise changing the subject using a bar model.

In this example, given the formula $a = 3c$, you can partition the part marked a to see that when c is the subject, $c = \frac{a}{3}$

Here you can see that $t = 3x + d$ can be written as $x = \frac{t - d}{3}$

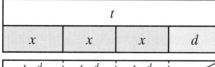

You can also change the subject by using inverse operations to **isolate** the new subject – to get it on its own.

Focus

Example 1
Make d the subject of the formula $c = 5d - 1$

$c = 5d - 1$ $+1 \qquad +1$	Add 1 to both sides of the formula.
$c + 1 = 5d$ $\div 5 \qquad \div 5$	Divide both sides of the formula by 5
$\frac{c + 1}{5} = d$	You could then rewrite in the form $d = \frac{c + 1}{5}$

Example 2
Make v the subject of the formula $k = 4a - \frac{bv}{2}$

$k = 4a - \frac{bv}{2}$ $+\frac{bv}{2} \qquad +\frac{bv}{2}$ $k + \frac{bv}{2} = 4a$	Add $\frac{bv}{2}$ to both sides of the formula. This makes the coefficient of the term with v positive.
$-k \qquad -k$ $\frac{bv}{2} = 4a - k$	Subtract k from both sides of the formula.

$\times 2$ $\times 2$ $bv = 2(4a - k)$	Multiply both sides of the formula by 2 Notice that you need brackets to show all terms on the right-hand side are multiplied by 2
$\div b$ $\div b$ $v = \frac{2(4a - k)}{b}$	Divide both sides of the formula by b.

Fluency

1 Make x the subject of each formula.

a) $r = x + t$

b) $v = z - x$

c) $w = \frac{x}{k}$

d) $a = \frac{m}{x}$

e) $p = 3x - 5$

f) $p = \frac{3}{2}gx$

g) $w = 12 - 7x$

h) $a = \frac{3f + x}{g}$

i) $y = \frac{3b - ax}{4}$

j) $d = 4x^2 + 7n$

k) $t = \sqrt{3x + 1}$

l) $y = \sqrt{5x} - h$

m) $z = \sqrt{\frac{x - 7}{3}}$

2 $t = \frac{a}{5} + 3$

a) Rearrange the formula to make a the subject.

b) Work out the value of t when $a = 12$

c) Work out the value of a when $t = 10$

3 A taxi has an initial fee of £3, and then costs 94p per mile travelled.

a) Write a formula for the total cost, C, of a taxi where m is the distance travelled in miles.

b) Rearrange your formula to make m the subject.

c) Work out, to the nearest mile, the distance travelled on a journey that costs £10.60

Further

1 The formula for the area of a triangle is $A = \frac{1}{2}bh$

Find the formula for the height of the triangle given the area and the length of the base. (2 marks)

2 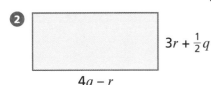 $3r + \frac{1}{2}q$

$4q - r$

a) Show that $P = 4r + 9q$, where P is the perimeter of the rectangle. (2 marks)

b) Rearrange $P = 4r + 9q$ to make q the subject. (2 marks)

3 The formula for the area of a circle is $A = \pi r^2$, where A is the area and r is the radius.

Write a formula to find the radius given the area A. (2 marks)

4 The formula to convert Celsius to Fahrenheit is $F = \frac{9C}{5} + 32$

Write a formula to convert Fahrenheit to Celsius by making C the subject of the formula. (2 marks)

5 The formula for the volume of a cone is $V = \frac{1}{3}\pi r^2 h$

a) Make h the subject of the formula. (2 marks)

b) Make r the subject of the formula. (2 marks)

c) Use your formula from part b) to work out the diameter of the base of a cone with a volume of 420 cm³ and a perpendicular height of 30 cm. Give your answer to 3 significant figures. (2 marks)

Foundations

Solve the equations.

a) $2x - 5 = 13$ b) $5 - 3x = 11$ c) $9 = -6 + 5x$

Facts

To solve equations with the unknown on both sides of the equation, you should balance the equation so that the unknown is only on one side. This can be shown using algebra tiles:

$2x + 3 = 5x + 1$

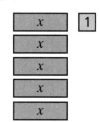

By subtracting $2x$ from both sides, the equation becomes $3 = 3x + 1$, which is much easier to solve.

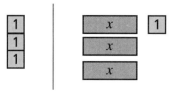

This can also be shown using a bar model:

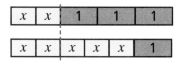

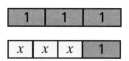

The two bars are the same length, as the two expressions they represent are equal.

Taking $2x$ from both bars again leaves you with the easier equation $3 = 3x + 1$

Focus

Example

Solve these equations.

a) $3x = x + 6$ b) $5y + 1 = 6y - 2$ c) $z + 1 = 4 - 5z$

a)	$3x = x + 6$ $\begin{array}{c} -x \quad -x \end{array}$ $2x = 6$	Subtract x from both sides of the equation.
	$\begin{array}{c} \div 2 \quad \div 2 \end{array}$ $x = 3$	Divide both sides by 2
b)	$5y + 1 = 6y - 2$ $\begin{array}{c} -5y \quad -5y \end{array}$ $1 = y - 2$	Subtract $5y$ from both sides of the equation.
	$\begin{array}{c} +2 \quad +2 \end{array}$ $y = 3$	Find the value of y by adding 2 to both sides.
c)	$z + 1 = 4 - 5z$ $\begin{array}{c} +5z \quad +5z \end{array}$ $6z + 1 = 4$	Add $5z$ to both sides of the equation. This means the remaining term in z will have a positive coefficient.
	$6z + 1 = 4$ $\begin{array}{c} -1 \quad -1 \end{array}$ $6z = 3$	Take 1 from both sides of the equation to isolate the unknown.
	$\begin{array}{c} \div 6 \quad \div 6 \end{array}$ $z = 0.5$	Divide both sides by 6

Fluency

1. Solve the equations.

   a) $4a + 7 = 5a$ b) $12b = 8b - 4$ c) $10 - 2c = 3c$

2. Solve the equations.

   a) $4d + 5 = 3d + 6$ b) $f + 2 = 7f - 10$ c) $2 + 7h = 3h - 10$

3. Solve the equations.

   a) $3j + 13 = 18 - 2j$ b) $-k + 3 = 3k - 1$ c) $3 - 2m = m - 9$

4. Solve the inequalities.

   a) $3p + 12 > p + 7$ b) $3p + 12 < 7p - 2$ c) $3p - 8 \geqslant 6p - 14$

5. a) Write down the inequality represented by the number line.

   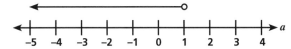

   b) The solution of which inequality is represented by the number line in part a)?

   A $5a + 2 \geqslant 4a + 1$ B $3a - 4 < 2a - 5$ C $2a - 6 > 3a - 7$

Further

1. Solve $14 - 3n = 11 - n$ (2 marks)

2. Solve $3(4p - 1) = 4p + 13$ (3 marks)

3. The square and the triangle have the same perimeter.

   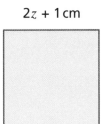

   2z + 1 cm

   2z − 1 cm   3z − 4 cm

   5z − 3 cm

   Find the value of the side length of the square.   (4 marks)

4. Four times a number with five more added is the same as one less than five times the number.

   Find the value of the number.   (3 marks)

5. Find the greatest integer value of x for which $10 - 3x > 17 - x$ (3 marks)

2.3 Laws of indices

Foundations

1 Simplify:

    a) $a \times a$ b) $b \times b \times b \times b \times b$ c) $c \times 2c \times 3c$

2 Calculate:

    a) 10^3 b) 7^2 c) 3^4

Facts

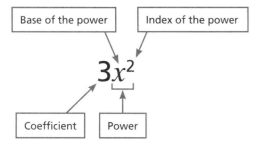

Base of the power	Index of the power

The plural of 'index' is 'indices'.

$$3x^2$$

Coefficient	Power

Terms involving indices can be added or subtracted only if they have the same power and the same base.

For example, $3x^4 + 2x^3 - x^4 + 11z^3 + 5x^3 \equiv 2x^4 + 7x^3 + 11z^3$

To multiply terms with indices that have the same base, you add the indices.

For example, $d^4 \times d^3 \equiv d^{4+3} \equiv d^7$

Similarly, when dividing, you subtract the indices.

For example, $m^8 \div m^2 \equiv m^{8-2} \equiv m^6$

If the base of a power is a power itself, for example $(x^4)^3$, multiply the indices together to get x^{12}.

Any number or variable to the power 0 is equal to 1

For example, $5^0 = 1$, $18^0 = 1$, $x^0 = 1$, $(9y)^0 = 1$

A power with a negative index can be rewritten as the reciprocal of the base with a positive index.

For example, $5^{-2} = \frac{1}{5^2} = \frac{1}{25}$ or $\left(\frac{3}{4}\right)^{-3} = \left(1 \div \left(\frac{3}{4}\right)\right)^3 = \left(\frac{4}{3}\right)^3 = \frac{64}{27}$

Focus

Example 1

Simplify:

    a) $5a^2 - 2a^2 + 7a^3$ b) $g^5 \times r^3 \times r \times g^2$ c) $\frac{k^{10}g^5}{k^2 g^3}$ d) $(2y^3)^5$

a) $3a^2 + 7a^3$	Collect terms that have the same power.
b) $g^5 \times r^3 \times r \times g^2 = g^5 \times g^2 \times r^3 \times r$ $= g^{5+2} \times r^{3+1} = g^7 r^4$ Note: $r = r^1$	Rewrite so the terms with g and the terms with r are together and add the powers.
c) $\frac{k^{10}g^5}{k^2 g^3} = k^{10-2}g^{5-3} = k^8 g^2$	Subtract the powers for both k and g.
d) $(2y^3)^5 = 2^5 \times (y^3)^5$ $= 32 \times y^{15}$ $= 32y^{15}$	Raise each part of the term in the brackets to the given power.

Example 2

Evaluate: a) 6^0 b) 3^{-2} c) $\left(\frac{1}{4}\right)^{-3}$

a) $6^0 = 1$	Any number raised to the power 0 is 1
b) $3^{-2} = \frac{1}{3^2} = \frac{1}{9}$	Rewrite as the reciprocal with a positive power.
c) $\left(\frac{1}{4}\right)^{-3} = 4^3 = 64$	The reciprocal of $\frac{1}{4}$ is 4

Fluency

1 Simplify:

   a) $3a^5 + a^5$ b) $5 \times 7b^3$ c) $6c^4 - 6c^3 + 4c^4 + 2c^3$

2 Simplify:

   a) $d^8 \times d^5$ b) $2f^3 \times f^2$ c) $g^7 \times g^4 \times g^{19}$ d) $4h^4 \times 3h^3$

   e) $9z^8 y \times 6y^2 z$ f) $-4x^3 n^{-2} \times 2x^{-1} n^7$ g) $-3t^{2.4} \times 8t^{3.6} \times -t^2$ h) $0.1f^{0.1} \times 10f^{0.9}$

3 Simplify:

   a) $j^{12} \div j^3$ b) $15k^6 \div 3k^2$ c) $\dfrac{m^{20} n^{12}}{n^{11} m^4}$ d) $\dfrac{20p^{32} q^7}{4p^8 q^{-1}}$

   e) $9r^{-10} \div 15r^{-2}$ f) $\dfrac{3d^6 \times 6d^4}{9d^4}$ g) $\dfrac{5y^{12} \times 9xy}{18y^{13} \times 3x^{10}}$ h) $\dfrac{15a^{36} \times 6b^{-10}}{36a^{-15} \times 2b^{-4}}$

4 Simplify:

   a) $(p^3)^4$ b) $(h^5)^6$ c) $(4f^4)^2$

5 Evaluate:

   a) $6^{11} \div 6^9$ b) 7^0 c) 2^{-3} d) $8^{-2} \times 4^3$

Further

1 Write $\dfrac{(a^2)^5}{(a^7)^3}$ as a single power of a.   (2 marks)

2 Simplify $\dfrac{3m^{12} n^{-5}}{15m^{-2} n^2}$ (2 marks)

3 $25^2 = 5^c$

   Work out the value of c.   (2 marks)

4 $r^5 \times r^2 = r^{10} \times r^w$

   Work out the value of w.   (2 marks)

5 Write $\dfrac{g^{\frac{1}{4}} \times g^{\frac{2}{3}}}{g^{\frac{1}{5}}}$ as a single power of g.   (3 marks)

6 Amina writes $2^5 \times 2^5 = 2^{10}$ because when the bases of the powers are the same, you add the indices.

   Rob writes $2^5 \times 2^5 = 4^5$ because when the indices of the powers are the same, you can multiply the bases.

   Show that both Amina and Rob are correct.   (2 marks)

7 Solve the equation $5^{2x-1} = 5^9 \times 5^{-2}$ (2 marks)

2.4 Expanding and factorising

Foundations

1 Expand:
     a) $2(a + 4)$
     b) $b(b - 3)$
     c) $2c(c + 3d)$

2 Factorise:
     a) $3f + 12$
     b) $g^2 - 5g$
     c) $5t^2 - 15tu$

Facts

Expanding a pair of brackets means to multiply them together. Using an area model can help.

Expand $(x + 2)(x + 3)$

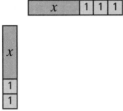
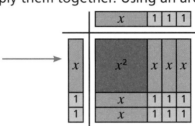

The area is $x^2 + 5x + 6$
So $(x + 2)(x + 3) \equiv x^2 + 5x + 6$

Factorising is the reverse process of expanding. We can use an area model again but work backwards:

Factorise $x^2 + 7x + 6$

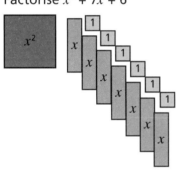
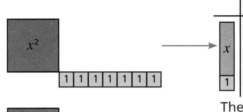
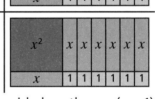

The side lengths are $(x + 1)(x + 6)$
So $x^2 + 7x + 6 \equiv (x + 1)(x + 6)$

> Not all seven 'x' tiles can be arranged into a rectangle using a 3 by 2 arrangement of the 6

In general, to factorise a quadratic of the form $x^2 + px + q$ you will need to find two values which have a product q and a sum p.

Factorising a quadratic such as $x^2 - 9$ is a special case, often known as **the difference of two squares**. The model on the right shows why $x^2 - 9$ factorised is $(x + 3)(x - 3)$

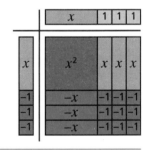

Focus

Example 1

Expand:
     a) $(x + 5)(x - 2)$
     b) $(y - 6)^2$

a) $(x + 5)(x - 2)$				Use an area model or a table. This helps to ensure that each term in the first pair of brackets is multiplied by each term in the other pair of brackets.
	$\times$	x	-2	
	x	x^2	$-2x$	
	5	$5x$	-10	

$x^2 + 5x - 2x - 10 \equiv x^2 + 3x - 10$	Add together each part of the area model or table and collect like terms where applicable.
b) $(y - 6)^2 \equiv (y - 6)(y - 6)$ $(y - 6)(y - 6) \equiv y^2 - 6y - 6y + 36$	This expression is '$y - 6$' all squared. Squaring means multiplying by itself, so here we can multiply $y - 6$ by $y - 6$
$y^2 - 6y - 6y + 36 \equiv y^2 - 12y + 36$	Collect like terms where applicable.

Example 2

Factorise:

a) $p^2 + 8p + 12$ b) $q^2 + 4q - 12$

a) $p^2 + 8p + 12$	Use a table, filling in the p^2 and constant term.
	The side lengths can be partly filled in with p as we know $p \times p = p^2$

×	p	
p	p^2	
		12

$2 \times 6 = 12$ and $2 + 6 = 8$	We now need to find a pair of values which multiply to make the constant (12) and sum to make the coefficient of p (8). The only possible values are 2 and 6

×	p	6
p	p^2	$6p$
2	$2p$	12

So $p^2 + 8p + 12 \equiv (p + 2)(p + 6)$	Write the quadratic as a product of the two factors.

b) $q^2 + 4q - 12$	Use a table, filling in the q^2 and constant term, and look for a pair of values which multiply to make the constant (–12) and sum to make the coefficient of q (4).

×	q	
q	q^2	
		–12

→

×	q	6
q	q^2	$6q$
–2	$-2q$	–12

$-2 \times 6 = -12$ and $-2 + 6 = 4$

So $q^2 + 4q - 12 \equiv (q - 2)(q + 6)$	Write the quadratic as a product of the two factors.

> You can check your answer is correct by expanding and simplifying to see if you get the expression you started with.

Fluency

1 Expand:

a) $(a + 3)(a + 8)$ b) $(b - 3)(b + 8)$ c) $(c + 3)(c - 8)$

d) $(d - 3)(d - 8)$ e) $(3 + f)(f - 8)$ f) $(3 - g)(g + 8)$

2 Factorise:

a) $h^2 + 6h + 5$ b) $j^2 + 9j + 20$ c) $k^2 - 7k + 10$

d) $l^2 + 10l - 24$ e) $m^2 - 3m - 18$ f) $n^2 + 15n - 34$

g) $x^2 - 36$ h) $y^2 - 100$ i) $25 - t^2$

3 Expand:

a) $(2p + 1)(p + 3)$ b) $(3q + 1)(q - 2)$ c) $(r - 4)(4r + 1)$

d) $(4s - 3)(3s - 4)$ e) $(t + 8)^2$ f) $(3u - 4)^2$

Further

1 Find an expanded expression for the area of the rectangle.   (2 marks)

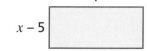

$2x + 7$

$x - 3$

2 Expand $(a + b)(c + d)$ (2 marks)

3 Show by expanding $(x + y)^2$ that $(x + y)^2 \neq x^2 + y^2$ (2 marks)

4 The expression for the area of the rectangle is $x^2 + 9x - 70$

Find an expression for the unknown side length.   (2 marks)

?

$x - 5$

5 Expand $(x + 5)(x + 4)(x + 3)$ (3 marks) | Expand any two brackets first and then multiply by the remaining bracket. |

6 Factorise $49a^2 - 81b^2$ (2 marks)

2.5 Algebraic arguments

Foundations

Write an expression for each statement.

a) 5 less than x

b) the sum of a, b and c

c) the product of a, b and c

d) the difference between t and r

Facts

We can represent even and odd numbers algebraically as $2n$ and $2n + 1$ respectively.

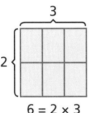

Even

$6 = 2 \times 3$

$2 \times n = 2n$

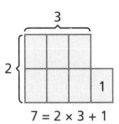

Odd

$7 = 2 \times 3 + 1$

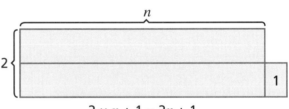

$2 \times n + 1 = 2n + 1$

We can use the same idea to represent a multiple of 3 ($3n$) or 4 ($4n$).

Focus

Example 1

Write an expression for:

a) a square number

b) one more than a multiple of 3

c) two less than a cube number

a)	For example, n^2	Any letter squared.
b)	For example, $3k + 1$	3 lots of any letter with 1 added to it.
c)	For example, $t^3 - 2$	Any letter cubed with 2 subtracted from it.

Example 2
a) Write an expression for the sum of any three consecutive odd numbers.
b) Prove, algebraically, that the sum of any three consecutive odd numbers is equal to three times the middle number.

a) Let the numbers be $2n + 1$, $2n + 3$ and $2n + 5$	Odd numbers are of the form $2n + 1$
	The next odd number is 2 greater, $2n + 1 + 2 = 2n + 3$
	The next after that is $2n + 3 + 2 = 2n + 5$
$2n + 1 + 2n + 3 + 2n + 5 \equiv 6n + 9$	Add together each of the expressions and collect like terms.
b) $6n + 9 \equiv 3(2n + 3)$ This is $3 \times (2n + 3)$, which is 3 times the middle number.	Factorise the expression using 3 as a common factor.

Fluency

1 Write algebraic expressions for the following descriptions.
   a) A multiple of 5
   b) A multiple of –3
   c) An even number
   d) One more than a multiple of 4
   e) Two less than a multiple of 9

2 a) q is an odd number.
      Write down the next odd number after q.
   b) r is a multiple of 3
      Write down the previous multiple of 3 before r.

3 a) Show that $6n$ is a multiple of 3
   b) Show that $20k$ is a multiple of 4
   c) Show that $15d - 10$ is a multiple of 5

4 A Fibonacci sequence has its first two terms as p and q.

> The next term in a Fibonacci sequence is the sum of the previous two terms.

   a) Write an expression for the fifth term of the sequence.
   b) Show that the sum of the first and fifth terms is equivalent to three times the third term.

Further

1 Show that the square of a multiple of 3 is always a multiple of 9   (2 marks)
2 Prove, algebraically, that the sum of any two consecutive numbers is odd.   (2 marks)
3 Prove, algebraically, that the product of any two consecutive numbers is even.   (2 marks)
4 Prove, algebraically, that any odd integer squared is 1 more than a multiple of 4   (3 marks)
5 Prove that $(n + 5)^2 - (n - 2)^2$ is always a multiple of 7   (3 marks)

2.6 Parallel lines

Foundations

Identify pairs of line segments that are parallel or perpendicular in this shape.

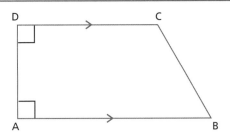

Facts

Straight lines with equations of the form $x = a$ are parallel to the y-axis.

Straight lines with equations of the form $y = a$ are parallel to the x-axis.

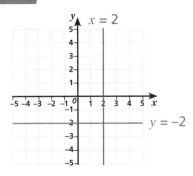

The **general equation of a straight line** can be expressed in the form $y = mx + c$, where m is the **gradient** and $(0, c)$ is the point at which the line **intercepts** the y-axis.

> More details about this form of an equation are given in unit 2.7

Lines that have the same gradient are parallel. For example, the two lines shown have equations $y = 2x + 1$ and $y = 2x - 4$ and both lines have a gradient of 2

$y = 2x + 1$ intercepts the y-axis at $(0, 1)$ and $y = 2x - 4$ intercepts the y-axis at $(0, -4)$.

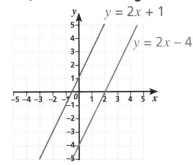

Focus

Example 1

Write the equation of a line that is parallel to:

a) $x = 4$ b) $y = -2$ c) $y = 2x$ d) $y = 2 - 3x$

a) For example, $x = -6$	An equation in the form of $x = a$ is a vertical line so any other vertical line will be parallel.
b) For example, $y = 5$	An equation in the form of $y = a$ is a horizontal line so any other horizontal line will be parallel.
c) For example, $y = 2x + 3$	$y = 2x$ has a gradient of 2 so any equation of the form $y = 2x + a$ will be parallel.
d) For example, $y = -3x + 1$	$y = 2 - 3x$ has a gradient of -3 so any equation of the form $y = -3x + a$ will be parallel.

Example 2

Find the pairs of parallel lines in this list.

$y = 2x$ $y = 5x + 2$ $y = 2x + 5$ $y = 2 - 5x$ $2y = -10x$ $y - 5x + 2 = 0$

$y = 2 - 5x \rightarrow y = -5x + 2$ $2y = -10x \rightarrow y = -5x$ $y - 5x + 2 = 0 \rightarrow y = 5x - 2$	Rearrange any equations that are not in the form $y = mx + c$ to make it easier to identify the gradient. Details about rearranging formulae are given in unit 2.1
$y = 2x$ and $y = 2x + 5$ $y = 5x + 2$ and $y - 5x + 2 = 0$ $y = 2 - 5x$ and $2y = -10x$	Match up the pairs of lines that have the same gradient.

Fluency

1 Write down the equation of a line parallel to each of these lines.

a) $x = 6$ b) $y = 0$ c) $y = 4x$ d) $y = x$

e) $y = -3x$ f) $y = 2x - 7$ g) $y = 10x + 4$ h) $y = -6x + 2$

2 Group the equations that are parallel to each other.

$y = 3x + 1$ $y = 2x - 3$ $y = 8x - 1$ $y = 3x - 1$

$y = 8 - 2x$ $y = 2x + 8$ $y = 2 + 8x$ $y = -3 - 2x$

3 Write down the equation of a line parallel to each of these lines.

a) $y = 1 + 4x$ b) $y = 1 - 4x$ c) $y = 4 - x$

d) $2y = 6x + 10$ e) $3y = 9x - 12$ f) $4y = 4x + 20$

4 Here are the equations of five straight lines:

A $y + 2x = 10$ B $2y + x = 10$ C $y = 2x + 7$ D $y = 7 - 2x$ E $2y = 7x + 10$

Two of the lines are parallel. Write down the two parallel lines.

Further

1 The line $y = 3x + 4$ crosses the y-axis at P.

a) What is the value of x at P? (1 mark) b) What is the value of y at P? (1 mark)

c) Write down the equation of a line parallel to $y = 3x + 4$ (1 mark)

2 Group the equations of lines that are parallel to each other.

$y = 4x + 10$ $4y = x - 10$ $y = 10 - 4x$ $3y = 12x$ $y = \frac{1}{4}x + 10$ $8y = 2x - 24$

$y + 4x = 100$ $2y = 8x + 16$ $5y = -20x$ (3 marks)

3 Two lines have equations $3y = 6x + 39$ and $y - 2x = 13$

Alex says that the two lines are parallel. Explain why Alex is wrong. (2 marks)

4 A line passes through the point $(0, -3)$. The gradient of the line is 5

Write down the equation of the line. (2 marks)

5 A straight line has equation $y = 7 - x$

a) Write down the gradient of the line. (1 mark)

b) Write down the coordinates of the point where the line crosses the y-axis. (1 mark)

2.7 Equation of a line

Foundations

1 Write down the gradient of each straight line. **a)** $y = 3x - 1$ **b)** $y = 2 - 5x$ **c)** $2y = 4x + 6$

2 Find the gradient of each line segment.

a) 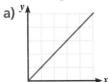 **b)** 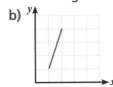 **c)** 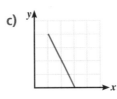 **d)**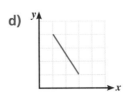

Facts

The equation of a straight line can be written in the form $y = mx + c$

The **gradient** of a straight line measures the steepness of the line and can be calculated if two points on the line are known.

The gradient of a line, m, can be found by calculating $\dfrac{\text{change in } y \text{ values}}{\text{change in } x \text{ values}}$

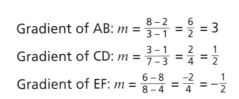

Gradient of AB: $m = \dfrac{8-2}{3-1} = \dfrac{6}{2} = 3$

Gradient of CD: $m = \dfrac{3-1}{7-3} = \dfrac{2}{4} = \dfrac{1}{2}$

Gradient of EF: $m = \dfrac{6-8}{8-4} = \dfrac{-2}{4} = -\dfrac{1}{2}$

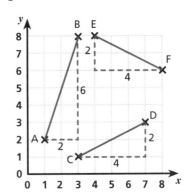

Focus

Example 1

Write the equation of a straight line that has:

a) a gradient of 4 and passes through (3, 7)

b) a gradient of –2 and passes through (14, 3)

c) a gradient of $\frac{1}{3}$ and passes through (2, 5)

a) $y = 4x + c$	Substitute the value of the gradient into $y = mx + c$
$7 = 4(3) + c$	Substitute (3, 7) using x as 3 and y as 7 and solve to find the value of c.
$7 = 12 + c$	
$c = -5$	
$y = 4x - 5$	Write the equation in the form $y = mx + c$
b) $y = -2x + c$	Substitute the value of the gradient into $y = mx + c$
$3 = -2(14) + c$	Substitute (14, 3) using x as 14 and y as 3 and solve to find the value of c.
$3 = -28 + c$	
$c = 31$	
$y = -2x + 31$	Write the equation in the form $y = mx + c$
	You could also write this as $y = 31 - 2x$

c) $y = \frac{1}{3}x + c$	Substitute the value of the gradient into $y = mx + c$
$5 = 2(\frac{1}{3}) + c$ $5 = \frac{2}{3} + c$ $c = \frac{13}{3}$	Substitute (2, 5) using x as 2 and y as 5 and solve to find the value of c.
$y = \frac{1}{3}x + \frac{13}{3}$	Write the equation in the form $y = mx + c$ You could also write this as $3y = x + 13$

Example 2

Find the equation of the line that passes through: a) (3, 2) and (–1, 14)   b) (–2, 20) and (13, 11)

a) $m = \frac{y_2 - y_1}{x_2 - x_1} = \frac{14 - 2}{(-1) - 3} = \frac{12}{-4} = -3$ $y = mx + c$	Find the difference between the y values of the two points and do the same with the x values. Divide the difference in the y values by the difference in the x values to find the gradient.
$2 = -3(3) + c$ $2 = -9 + c$ $c = 11$	Substitute one of the points into the equation with gradient –3 to find the value of c.
$y = -3x + 11$	Write the equation in the form $y = mx + c$
b) $m = \frac{y_2 - y_1}{x_2 - x_1} = \frac{11 - 20}{13 - (-2)} = \frac{-9}{15} = -\frac{3}{5}$ $y = mx + c$	Find the difference between the y values of the two points and do the same with the x values. Divide the difference in the y values by the difference in the x values to find the gradient.
$20 = -\frac{3}{5}(-2) + c$ $20 = \frac{6}{5} + c$ $c = \frac{94}{5}$	Substitute one of the points into the equation with gradient $-\frac{3}{5}$ to find the value of c.
$y = -\frac{3}{5}x + \frac{94}{5}$	Write the equation in the form $y = mx + c$. You could also write this as $5y = -3x + 94$

Fluency

1 Write the equation of the line with:

   a) a gradient of 3 that goes through (1, 2)   b) a gradient of 1 that goes through (–3, –8)

   c) a gradient of –2 that goes through (–4, 7)   d) a gradient of –10 that goes through (18, 40)

2 Write down an equation of the straight line that goes through:

   a) (2, 3) and (4, 13)   b) (–2, 3) and (–4, –13)   c) (–2, 3) and (4, –15)

Further

1 Write the equation of the line passing through (–12, 5) with gradient $\frac{1}{4}$ (2 marks)

2 Write down the equation of the line passing through (10, 12) and (14, 15)

   Give your answer in the form $ax + by + c = 0$ where a, b and c are integers. (3 marks)

3 Write down the equation of the line that passes through (2, 7) and is parallel to the line shown in the graph. (3 marks)

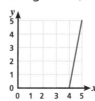

4 Line l has a gradient of 5 and passes through (–3, –21) and (2, q)

   Find the value of q. (3 marks)

2.8 Plotting more complex functions

Foundations

Use a table of values to plot the graph of $y = 3x - 4$

Facts

An equation like $y = 3x + 5$ has a straight line graph and is called a **linear** function. | See unit 2F1 for more details. |

A function where the greatest power of x is x^2 is called a **quadratic**. The graphs of quadratic functions are U-shaped and symmetrical. If the x^2 term is negative, the graph has an inverted U-shape.

Cubic functions are functions where x^3 is the greatest power of x. For example, $y = x^3 + 7$

Reciprocal functions are of the form $y = \frac{k}{x}$

Exponential functions take the form $y = a^x$

The shapes of these graphs are explored in this unit.

Focus

Example 1

Plot the graph of $y = x^3 + x$ for $-2 \leqslant x \leqslant 2$

x	-2	-1	0	1	2
$y = x^3 + x$	-10	-2	0	2	10

Complete a table of values to find coordinates of points on the curve.

In an exam, you will usually be given a partly filled table of values to complete.

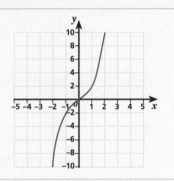

Plot the coordinates from your table of values. Then join the points with a smooth curve.

Example 2

Plot the graph of $y = \frac{1}{x}$ for $-4 \leqslant x \leqslant 4$

x	-4	-2	-1	1	2	4
$y = \frac{1}{x}$	$-\frac{1}{4}$	$-\frac{1}{2}$	-1	1	$\frac{1}{2}$	$\frac{1}{4}$

Complete a table of values to find coordinates of points on the curve.

| You cannot work out $1 \div 0$ so the point where $x = 0$ is left out. |

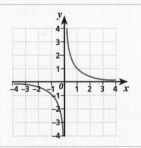

Plot the coordinates from your table of values. Then join the points with two smooth curves.

Notice that the graph has two distinct sections that never meet the x or y axes.

Fluency

1 a) Complete the table of values for $y = x^3 - 2x$

x	−2	−1	0	1	2
$y = x^3 - 2x$					

b) Plot the graph of $y = x^3 - 2x$ for $-2 \leqslant x \leqslant 2$

2 a) Complete the table of values for $y = \frac{2}{x}$

x	−4	−3	−2	−1	1	2	3	4
$y = \frac{2}{x}$								

b) Plot the graph of $y = \frac{2}{x}$ for $-4 \leqslant x \leqslant 4$

3 Use a table of values to help plot the graph of $y = 2^x$ for $-3 \leqslant x \leqslant 3$

4 Match the graphs A, B, C and D to their equations.

Equation	Graph
$y = 3x + 5$	
$y = \frac{3}{x}$	
$y = 5 - 3x$	
$y = x^2 - 4$	

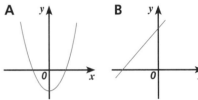

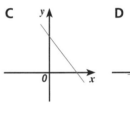

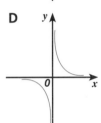

Further

1 The graph shows the curve $y = a^x$

Use the coordinates marked to work out the value of a.   (2 marks)

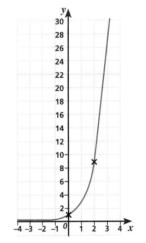

2 a) Complete the table of values.   (2 marks)

x	−3	−2	−1	1	2	3
$y = \frac{1}{x^2}$						

b) Plot the graph of $y = \frac{1}{x^2}$ (2 marks)

c) Use your graph to estimate the solution to $\frac{1}{x^2} = 0.5$ (1 mark)

3 A type of bacteria grows at a rate modelled by the function $f(t) = 2a^t$ where a is the starting number of bacteria and t is the number of hours.

Complete the table.   (3 marks)

Time (hours)	0	0.5	1	1.5	2	4	10
Number of bacteria (thousands)						162	

2.9 Roots and turning points

Foundations

Factorise: **a)** $x^2 + 7x + 10$ **b)** $x^2 + 3x - 10$ **c)** $x^2 - 3x - 10$

Facts

The **intercepts** on a graph are the points where a line or a curve crosses the axes. They are known as the **x-intercepts** and the **y-intercept**.

Turning points are where a graph reaches a **maximum** or a **minimum value**.

The **roots** of an equation such as $y = ax^2 + bx + c$ are the value(s) of x when $y = 0$. These correspond to the point or points at which the graph of $y = ax^2 + bx + c$ crosses the x-axis, i.e. the x-intercept(s). They are the same as the **solutions** of the equation $ax^2 + bx + c = 0$

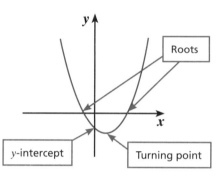

You can also solve a quadratic equation algebraically. This method is covered in unit 2.11

Focus

Example 1

Use the graph to identify the roots, y-intercept and the turning point of the equation $y = x^2 + 3x - 4$

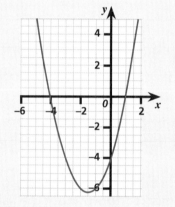

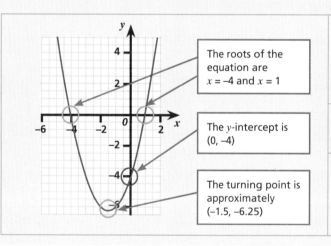

The roots of the equation are $x = -4$ and $x = 1$	Find the x-intercepts. Notice that this quadratic factorises to $(x + 4)(x - 1)$. The x values of the intercepts are the roots of the equation.
The y-intercept is $(0, -4)$	The y-intercept is the coordinate where the curve crosses the y-axis.
The turning point is approximately $(-1.5, -6.25)$	The turning point of the curve is the minimum point. The value of y decreases up to the turning point and then increases.

Example 2

Work out the roots of the equation $y = x^2 - 5x - 14$

$x^2 - 5x - 14 = 0$	The roots of the equation are where $y = 0$
$(x + 2)(x - 7) = 0$	Factorise the quadratic.
Either $x + 2 = 0$ or $x - 7 = 0$	Solve the resulting linear equations to find x.
So $x = -2$ or $x = 7$	

Fluency

For each graph, write down:

i) the roots

ii) the y-intercept

iii) the coordinates of the turning point.

a)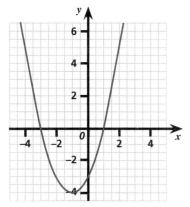

b)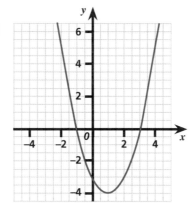

c)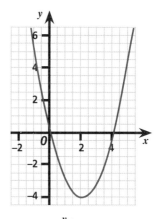

d)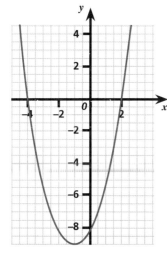

e)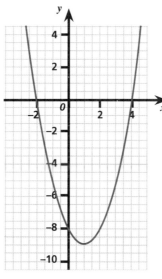

f)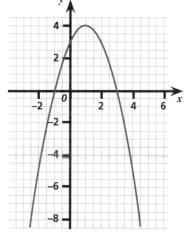

Further

1 a) On a grid, draw a graph of $y = 5x - x^2$ for values of x from -1 to 5 (2 marks)

b) Use your graph to find an estimate for the turning point of the graph $y = 5x - x^2$ (1 mark)

c) Solve the equation $5x - x^2 = 0$ (2 marks)

d) Find estimates of the solutions of the equation $5x - x^2 = 3$ (2 marks) | Add the line $y = 3$ to your graph.

2 a) Use a graph to estimate the roots of $x^2 + 3x - 1 = 0$ (3 marks)

b) By adding a straight line to your graph, find estimates of the roots of $x^2 + 3x - 3 = 0$ (2 marks)

2.10 Simultaneous equations

Foundations

Solve: **a)** $4(x - 5) = 22$ **b)** $3y - 5 = 7y + 14$

Facts

Simultaneous equations involve two variables. To solve a pair of simultaneous equations, the first step is to substitute, add or subtract to get an equation in only one variable.

These bar models show the equations

$$3h + 2j = 14$$
$$h + 2j = 10$$

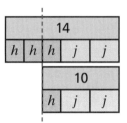

By 'cutting off' the ends of the bars, you can see that $2h = 4$

This result can also be found by subtracting the equations term by term.

You can solve $2h = 4$ to give $h = 2$ and then substitute this into either of the given equations to find the value of j ($= 4$).

Focus

Example 1

Solve the simultaneous equations

$$y = x + 2 \qquad \text{(A)}$$
$$y + 3x = 14 \qquad \text{(B)}$$

$x + 2 + 3x = 14$	Substitute $x + 2$ for y in equation B.
$4x + 2 = 14$	Simplify the equation by collecting like terms.
$4x + 2 = 14$ $-2 \qquad -2$	Subtract 2 from both sides.
$4x = 12$ $\div 4 \quad \div 4$ $x = 3$	Divide by 4
$y = 3 + 2$ $y = 5$	Substitute $x = 3$ into equation A to find the value of y.
So $x = 3$, $y = 5$	You can check your result in equation (B). $5 + 3 \times 3 = 14$ as required.
	The solution to a pair of simultaneous equations represents the intersection of two lines; in this example, lines A and B cross at (3, 5).

This is the **substitution** method because you substitute one variable in place of another.

Example 2

Solve the simultaneous equations

$$h + j = 12$$
$$5h + 2j = 39$$

$h + j = 12$ (A) $5h + 2j = 39$ (B)	Label the equations to help make your workings clear.
$2h + 2j = 24$ (C)	Multiply equation A by 2 to create equation C so the coefficients of one of the variables (j) are the same in the two equations.
$3h = 15$ (B) − (C) $h = 5$	Subtract equation C from equation B to eliminate the variable j, as $2j - 2j = 0$. Solve the resulting equation to find h.
$5 + j = 12$ $j = 7$	Substitute $h = 5$ into equation A to find the value of j.

Example 3

Solve the simultaneous equations
$$12x - 5y = -22$$
$$-8x + 4y = 16$$

$12x - 5y = -22$ (A) $-8x + 4y = 16$ (B) (A) × 2 = (C) (B) × 3 = (D)	Multiply equation A by 2 and equation B by 3 to generate coefficients of x you can eliminate. Label the new equations C and D.
$+\begin{array}{r} 24x - 10y = -44 \text{ (C)} \\ -24x + 12y = 48 \text{ (D)} \end{array}+$ $2y = 4$ $y = 2$	Add equations C and D to eliminate the x variable (as $-24x + 24x = 0$) Solve for y.
$-8x + 4(2) = 16$ $-8x + 8 = 16$ $\quad -8 \qquad\quad -8$ $-8x = 8$ $x = -1$	Substitute $y = 2$ into equation B to find the value of x. You can substitute $y = 2$ into any of the equations.

Examples 2 and 3 show the **elimination** method because you adjust the equations to eliminate one of the two variables.

Fluency

1 Solve the simultaneous equations by substitution.

  a) $y = x - 1$
     $y + 4x = 15$

  b) $y = x - 1$
     $3y + 4x = 10$

  c) $x = y - 1$
     $3y - 4x = 10$

2 Solve the simultaneous equations by elimination.

  a) $2a + 4b = 20$
     $7a + 4b = 45$

  b) $2a + 4b = 20$
     $7a - 4b = 25$

  c) $2a - 3b = 17$
     $2a + 5b = 29$

3 Solve the simultaneous equations by elimination.

  a) $5h + 2j = 4$
     $2h + 3j = 3.8$

  b) $5h + 4j = 20$
     $2h + 3j = 3.8$

  c) $2h + 4j = -22$
     $5h - 6j = 9$

Further

1 Is $p = 5$ and $r = 3$ a solution to these simultaneous equations?

  $p = 8 - r$ $\qquad$ $2p - r = 4$

  Give a reason for your answer.   (1 mark)

2 A plumber charges a price per hour (h) and a fixed cost (c).

  A job that takes 5 hours costs £155

  A job that takes 8 hours costs £230

  a) Find the hourly rate and the fixed cost the plumber charges.   (4 marks)

  b) Calculate the cost of a job that takes 10 hours to complete.   (1 mark)

  > Write a pair of simultaneous equations in h and c first.

3 The cost of 3 pens and 2 rubbers is £3.24

  The cost of 2 pens and 2 rubbers is £2.76

  Find the cost of 8 pens and 6 rubbers.   (5 marks)

2.11 Solving quadratic equations by factorisation

Foundations

1. Solve these equations.

   a) $x + 4 = 0$ b) $x - 4 = 0$ c) $2x - 4 = 0$

2. Factorise these expressions.

   a) $x^2 + 3x + 2$ b) $x^2 - 3x - 4$ c) $x^2 - 5x + 4$

Facts

Quadratic equations are equations where the greatest power of the variable is 2

Examples of quadratic equations are $x^2 + 3x + 2 = 0$, $p^2 - 9 = 27$ and $m^2 - 2m = 3$

Quadratic equations have either zero, one or two solutions.

One method to solve quadratic equations is to use **factorisation** – see the examples below. Factorising quadratics is covered in unit 2.4

Focus

Example 1
Solve the equation $x^2 - 5x + 4 = 0$

$x^2 - 5x + 4 = 0$	
$(x - 4)(x - 1) = 0$	Factorise the quadratic expression.
Either $x - 4 = 0$ or $x - 1 = 0$	If the product of the two brackets is zero, one of the brackets must equal zero.
So $x = 4$ or $x = 1$	Solve the two linear equations formed to find the values of x.

Example 2
Solve the equation $x^2 + 11x = -30$

$x^2 + 11x = -30$ $+30 \qquad\quad +30$ $x^2 + 11x + 30 = 0$	In order to solve a quadratic, it must first be rearranged so the quadratic expression is equal to zero. So add 30 to both sides.
$(x + 6)(x + 5) = 0$	Factorise the quadratic expression.
Either $x + 6 = 0$ or $x + 5 = 0$	If the product of the two brackets is zero, one of the brackets must equal zero.
$x = -6$ or $x = -5$	Solve the two linear equations formed to find the values of x.

Example 3
The area of the rectangle is 36 cm²
Find the dimensions of the rectangle.

$(x + 2)$ cm

$(x - 3)$ cm

Area of the rectangle = 36 cm² Area of the rectangle = $(x + 2)(x - 3)$	Form an equation for the area of the rectangle using area = length × width
Therefore: $(x + 2)(x - 3) = 36$	
$x^2 - x - 6 = 36$	Expand the brackets.

$x^2 - x - 42 = 0$	Subtract 36 to make the equation equal to zero.
$(x - 7)(x + 6) = 0$	Factorise the quadratic expression.
Either $x - 7 = 0$ or $x + 6 = 0$	Allow each bracket to equal zero and solve.
$x = 7$ or $x = -6$ (rejected) So $x = 7$	You can discard $x = -6$ as a solution in this case because you are finding a length, so negative solutions are not possible.
Length: 9 cm Width: 4 cm	Substitute $x = 7$ to find the dimensions.

Fluency

1 Solve these equations.

    a) $(x - 5)(x + 1) = 0$ b) $(4 + x)(x - 6) = 0$ c) $x(x - 5) = 0$

2 Solve these equations by factorising.

    a) $g^2 + 4g + 3 = 0$ b) $g^2 + 4g + 4 = 0$ c) $g^2 - 4g + 3 = 0$

3 Solve these equations by factorising.

    a) $m^2 - 3m - 10 = 0$ b) $m^2 + 3m - 10 = 0$ c) $m^2 - 25 = 0$

4 Rearrange and solve these quadratic equations.

    a) $x^2 + 4x = 117$ b) $x^2 - 7x - 12 = 6$ c) $x^2 - 8x + 6 = 2x - 3$

Further

1 The area of the rectangle is 40 cm²

    Find the dimensions of the rectangle.   (3 marks)

x cm

(*x* 3) cm

2 Jakub solves the equation $x^2 + 3x = 10$

    a) Explain Jakub's mistake.   (1 mark)

    b) Work out the correct solutions to the equation.   (2 marks)

Jakub's solution:
$$x^2 + 3x = 10$$
$$x(x + 3) = 10$$
$$x + 3 = 10 \text{ or } x = 10$$
$$\text{So } x = 7 \text{ or } x = 10$$

3 Show algebraically that the equation $x^2 + 10x + 25 = 0$ has only one solution.   (2 marks)

4 The area of the triangle is equal to 14 mm²

    Find the value of x.   (4 marks)

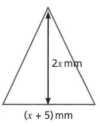

2*x* mm

(*x* + 5) mm

5 The trapezium has an area of 36 m²

    a) Show that $x^2 + 5x - 50 = 0$ (3 marks)

    b) Hence or otherwise, find the difference between the lengths of the parallel sides.   (2 marks)

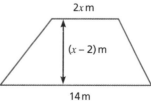

2*x* m

(*x* – 2) m

14 m

Foundations

Solve: **a)** $3x + 5 \leqslant 14$ **b)** $2x - 7 > 12$ **c)** $3x + 5 < 14 + 2x$ **d)** $2x - 7 \geqslant 12 - 3x$

Facts

An **inequality** compares values. Unlike equations, inequalities do not have a single solution but have **solution sets**. These solution sets can be represented on **number lines**.

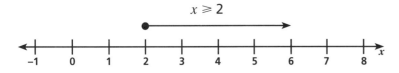

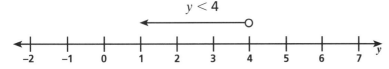

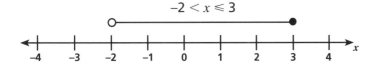

A filled circle shows that a value is included in the solution set and an open circle shows that a value is not included in the solution set.

Focus

Example 1
Represent the solution to $2x - 3 \geqslant 7$ on a number line.

$2x - 3 \geqslant 7$
    $+3$ $+3$
     $2x \geqslant 10$
    $\div 2$ $\div 2$
     $x \geqslant 5$
	Solve the inequality.

 number line showing $x \geqslant 5$ with filled circle at 5	Show the solution set on a number line. 5 is included in the solution set, so the circle is filled.

Example 2
a) Describe the inequality shown on the number line.

b) List all the integer solutions.

a) $-3 < x \leqslant 5$	Notice that although 5 is included in the solution set, -3 is not.
b) The integer solutions are $-2, -1, 0, 1, 2, 3, 4, 5$	The integer solutions are the whole numbers included in the range of the inequality. 0 is an integer and is included in this set.

Example 3
Show the solution to $-2 \leqslant 2x + 3 < 5$ on a number line.

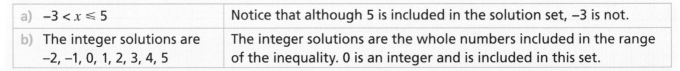

$-2 \leqslant 2x + 3$ $-3 \quad\quad -3$ $-5 \leqslant 2x$ $\div 2 \quad \div 2$ $-2.5 \leqslant x$	$2x + 3 < 5$ $-3 \quad -3$ $2x < 2$ $\div 2 \quad \div 2$ $x < 1$	Solve by splitting into two inequalities, $-2 \leqslant 2x + 3$ and $2x + 3 < 5$, and solving them separately.
$-2.5 \leqslant x < 1$ 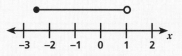		Write your answer as a single inequality and show on a number line.

Fluency

1 Show these inequalities on a number line.   **a)** $x > 3$ **b)** $3 < x$ **c)** $x > -3$

2 Show these dual inequalities on a number line.   **a)** $-2 < x \leqslant 5$ **b)** $-5 \leqslant x < 2$ **c)** $-5 \leqslant x \leqslant -2$

3 Write down the inequalities shown on these number lines.

a)

b)

c)
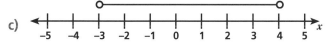

4 Write down the possible integer solutions for these inequalities.

   a) $-5 \leqslant x \leqslant -2$ **b)** $-2 < x \leqslant 3$ **c)** $-3 < x < 4$

Further

1 Match the inequalities and their number lines.   (2 marks)

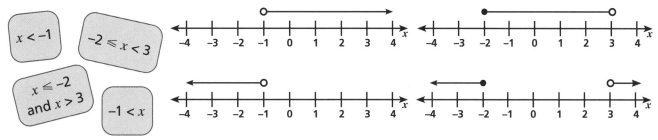

$x < -1$ $-2 \leqslant x < 3$ $x \leqslant -2$ and $x > 3$ $-1 < x$

2 a) Tiff states that the inequality shown is $-2 \leqslant x \leqslant 4$

   Explain why Tiff is incorrect.   (1 mark)

   b) What inequality does the number line show?   (1 mark)

3 a) Which of the following inequalities could the number line represent?

   $2x + 5 \leqslant 9$ $2x - 7 < -3$ $3x - 7 \leqslant -1$ (2 marks)

   b) The equation below has the same solution set as the inequality shown in part a).

     $5x + 6 \leqslant z$ Work out the value of z.   (2 marks)

2.13 Non-linear sequences

Foundations

A sequence starts 7, 10, 13, 16, ...

a) Find the rule for the nth term of the sequence.

b) Find the 100th term of the sequence.

c) Show that 60 is not a term in the sequence.

Facts

Non-linear sequences do not have constant differences.

The rule for a **quadratic sequence** will include an n^2 or an^2 term such as $n^2 + 2$, $n^2 - 3n$ or $2n^2 + 2n - 3$
The square numbers (1, 4, 19, 16, ...) form a quadratic sequence given by n^2, and the triangular numbers (1, 3, 6, 10, 15, ...) are given by $\frac{1}{2}n(n + 1)$

In a **Fibonacci sequence**, the next term is found by adding the previous two terms.
For example, 1, 1, 2, 3, 5, 8, 13, ... or 3, 4, 7, 11, 18, ...

Geometric sequences are sequences where each term is found by multiplying the previous term by a **constant multiplier**. For example, 2, 4, 8, 16, 32, ... (multiply by 2 each time) or 81, 27, 9, 3, 1, $\frac{1}{3}$, ... (multiply by $\frac{1}{3}$ each time).

Focus

Example 1

a) Generate the first five terms of the sequence $n^2 + n + 8$

b) Find the value of the 50th term in the sequence.

a) $n = 1$: $1^2 + 1 + 8 = 10$	Substitute the values 1–5 into the expression to find the terms of the sequence.
$n = 2$: $2^2 + 2 + 8 = 14$	
$n = 3$: $3^2 + 3 + 8 = 20$	
$n = 4$: $4^2 + 4 + 8 = 28$	
$n = 5$: $5^2 + 5 + 8 = 38$	
The first five terms are 10, 14, 20, 28 and 38	
b) When $n = 50$, $50^2 + 50 + 8 = 2558$	For the 50th term, $n = 50$

Example 2

The first two terms of a Fibonacci sequence are a and b. Find an expression for the fifth term.

1st term is a, 2nd term is b.	To generate the terms of a Fibonacci sequence, you add the previous two terms.
3rd term is equal to the 1st term + 2nd term	
3rd term: $a + b$	Generate each expression until you have the fifth term.
4th term is equal to the 2nd term + 3rd term	
4th term: $b + a + b = a + 2b$	
5th term is equal to the 3rd term + 4th term	
5th term: $a + b + a + 2b = 2a + 3b$	

Example 3

A geometric sequence has a first term of 3 and a common ratio of 2

a) Generate the first five terms of the sequence.

b) Find the eighth term of the sequence.

c) State whether 503 is a term in the sequence. Explain your reasoning.

a)	1st term: 3	The first term is 3
	2nd term: 3 × 2 = 6	The term-to-term rule for the sequence is
	3rd term: 6 × 2 = 12	multiply by 2 because the common ratio is 2
	4th term: 12 × 2 = 24	
	5th term: 24 × 2 = 48	
	The first five terms are 3, 6, 12, 24 and 48	
b)	8th term: 48 × 2 × 2 × 2 or 48 × 2³ = 384	Keep multiplying by 2 to find the eighth term.
c)	503 is not a term in the sequence because all the terms after the first are even numbers. This pattern will not change because you continue to multiply by 2 and therefore the numbers in the sequence will continue to be even.	

Fluency

1. Find the fourth term of the sequences given by each of these rules.

   a) $n^2 + 5$ = 21   b) $\dfrac{n^2 + 5}{2}$ = 10.5   c) $n(n + 5)$ = 36

2. Generate the first five terms of each sequence.

   a) $n^2 + n + 1$ b) $n^2 - n - 1$ c) $(n + 1)(n - 1)$

3. The first two terms of a Fibonacci sequence are a and $3a$

   Write expressions for the: a) third term   b) seventh term   c) tenth term

4. The first two terms of a Fibonacci sequence are $2a + 3$ and $3b$

   a) Write expressions for the next three terms.

   b) Write an expression for the seventh term of the sequence.

5. A geometric sequence has a common ratio of 2 and a first term of 5

   Show that the eighth term of the sequence is 640

Further

1. a) Use the rule $-3n(n - 5)$ to complete the table of results.   (2 marks)

Position (n)	1	2	3	4	5
Term		18	18		

   b) Show that the sum of the sixth and seventh terms of the sequence is −60   (2 marks)

2. The nth term rule for the sequence of triangular numbers is $\frac{1}{2}n(n + 1)$

   Show that the eleventh triangular number is 66   (2 marks)

3. The cards show a Fibonacci sequence with missing terms.

   (…)   ($3n - 2$)   ($n + 1$)   (…)   (…)

   a) Write expressions for the missing terms in the sequence.   (2 marks)

   b) If $n = 5$, show that the seventh term of the sequence is equal to 69   (2 marks)

4. A geometric sequence starts   …, $4ar$, …, $4ar^3$, …

   a) Write expressions for the missing terms above.   (2 marks)

   b) The second term of the sequence is 3, the fourth term is 27, and all the terms are positive.

   Find the values of a and r.   (3 marks)

Facts

A **ratio** compares two or more quantities.

There are five blue counters and four yellow counters, so the ratio of blue counters to yellow counters is 5 : 4, which is read as 'five to four'.

The ratio of yellow counters to blue counters is 4 : 5

You can also represent this as a bar model:

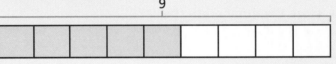

These diagrams show that 3 : 12 and 1 : 4 are **equivalent** ratios. In both cases, for every red cube there are four grey cubes.

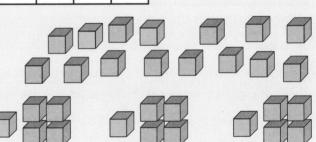

1 : 4 is the simplest integer form of the ratio.

The most efficient way of simplifying a ratio is to divide the numbers by the highest common factor.

$\div 8 \left(\begin{array}{c} 16 : 40 \\ 2 : 5 \end{array} \right) \div 8$

6 cm : 300 mm : 1 m
60 mm : 300 mm : 1000 mm
60 : 300 : 1000 $\div 20 \div 20 \div 20$
3 : 15 : 50

> Make sure the units are the same before simplifying the ratio.

Although you usually write a ratio using integers, you may be asked to write it in the form 1 : n or n : 1
In these cases, n could be a decimal.

$\div 5 \left(\begin{array}{c} 5 : 4 \\ 1 : 0.8 \end{array} \right) \div 5$ $\div 4 \left(\begin{array}{c} 5 : 4 \\ 1.25 : 1 \end{array} \right) \div 4$

When **sharing in a ratio**, a bar model is very helpful to make the structure of the problem clear.

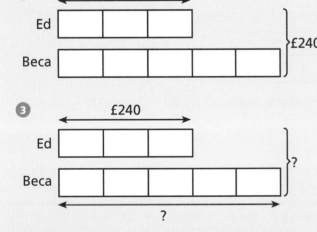

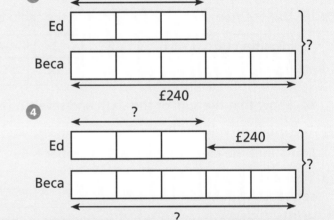

In model 1, £240 is the total amount Ed and Beca are going to share between them. 8 parts = £240

In model 2, £240 is Beca's share. 5 parts = £240

In model 3, £240 is Ed's share. 3 parts = £240

In model 4, £240 is the difference between Ed's part and Beca's part. 2 parts = £240

Scales on a map are an example of ratio.
For example, 1 : 40 000 means every one unit
on the map represents 40 000 units in real life.
Double number lines can be useful to
show connections in ratio problems.

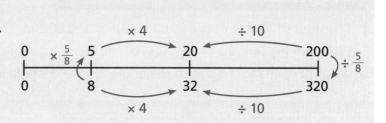

Practice

1. Write each ratio in its simplest form.

   a) 12 : 30   b) 500 : 60   c) 270 : 810   d) 2 kg : 800 g

2. A bag contains red counters and green counters.

   $\frac{3}{7}$ of the counters are red.

   Write down the ratio of red counters to green counters in the bag.

3. A box contains milk chocolates, dark chocolates and white chocolates.

   The number of milk chocolates is four times the number of dark chocolates.

   The number of dark chocolates is twice the number of white chocolates.

   What fraction of the chocolates are dark chocolates?

4. Mario and Huda share £300 in the ratio 2 : 3

   How much do they each get?

5. Amina and Seb share some money in the ratio 3 : 5

   Seb gets £80 more than Amina.

   How much money did they share?

6. Use the fact that 5 miles is about 8 kilometres to convert:

   a) 30 miles to kilometres   b) 160 kilometres to miles

7. AC is a straight line.

   The length of AB is one quarter the length of BC.

   AC = 60 cm

   Find the length of BC.

8. A map is drawn to a scale of 1 : 50 000

   Two towns are 30 cm apart on the map.

   Work out the actual distance between the two towns. Give your answer in kilometres.

9. Write the ratio 8 : 5 in the form:

   a) 1 : n b) n : 1

10. In a park, the ratio of adults to children is 1 : 3

    The ratio of male children to female children is 2 : 3

    What fraction of the people in the park are female children?

3.1 Similar shapes

Foundations

a) The sides of a triangle are 40 mm, 60 mm and 80 mm. The triangle is enlarged by scale factor 3
   What are the lengths of the sides of the enlarged triangle?

b) What happens to the size of the angles of the triangle in the enlargement?

Facts

Two shapes are said to be **similar** if their corresponding sides are in the same ratio. This ratio can be represented as the **scale factor** of enlargement between the two shapes.

Shape A and shape B are similar because each length in shape A has been multiplied by 3 to give the corresponding length in shape B.

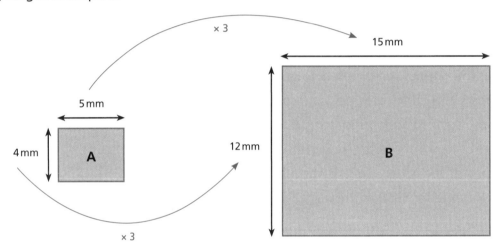

Focus

Example 1

These two figures are similar.

a) Calculate the lengths marked p and q.

b) Write down the size of the angle marked x.

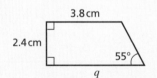 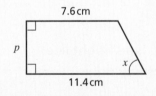

a) $7.6 \div 3.8 = 2$ The scale factor is 2	To find the scale factor, you divide the length of a side in the image by the corresponding side in the original shape.
$p = 2.4 \times 2 = 4.8$ cm	Since the shapes are similar, the side lengths are all enlarged by the same scale factor.
$q \times 2 = 11.4$ $q = 11.4 \div 2 = 5.7$ cm	You know that when q is multiplied by 2, the answer is 11.4 So you can work backwards to find q.
b) $x = 55°$	The angles in a shape don't change when the shape is enlarged.

Example 2
Triangles ABC and DEF are similar.
Work out the length of the side AB.

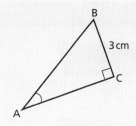
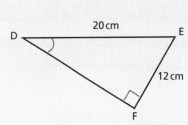

Scale factor = $\frac{EF}{BC} = \frac{12}{3} = 4$	Work out the scale factor of the enlargement from triangle ABC to triangle DEF. EF and BC correspond as they are both opposite the angle labelled with an arc.
AB = 20 ÷ 4 　 = 5 cm	Side AB corresponds to DE and ABC is the smaller triangle, so AB = DE ÷ 4 In the same way, DF = AC × 4 as DEF is the larger of the two triangles.

Fluency

1 Rectangles A and B are similar.

　a) Work out the scale factor of enlargement from A to B.

　b) Work out the length, l, of rectangle B.

2 A £5 note is a rectangle with a width of 65 mm and a length of 125 mm.

　A £20 note is a rectangle with a width of 73 mm and a length of 139 mm.

　Are the notes mathematically similar?

3 Explain why triangles TUS and XYZ are similar.

4 Quadrilaterals ABCD and PQRS are similar.

　Work out the lengths of:

　a) BC　　　　　b) RS

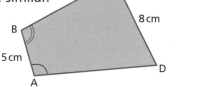
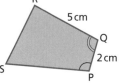

Further

1 The diagram shows a pair of similar triangles.

　Work out the lengths marked x and y.　(4 marks)

> See more about pairs of triangles that are similar in unit 4.9

2 Work out the length of:

　a) AB　(1 mark)

　b) BC　(1 mark)

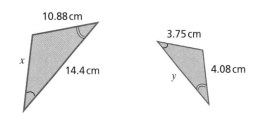

3 A shape is enlarged by scale factor 3

　Seb thinks the area of the new shape will be six times that of the original shape.

　Explain why Seb is wrong and state the correct area scale factor.　(2 marks)

3.2 Converting compound units

White Rose Maths

Foundations

Complete these conversions.

a) 1 kilometre = ... metres   b) 1 kilogram = ... grams   c) 1 hour = ... seconds

Facts

To convert units of area or volume, you can write out calculations. For example:

$1\,cm^2 = 1\,cm \times 1\,cm = 10\,mm \times 10\,mm = 100\,mm^2$

$1\,m^3 = 1\,m \times 1\,m \times 1\,m = 100\,cm \times 100\,cm \times 100\,cm = 1\,000\,000\,cm^3$

Compound units are used to describe measures that involve a rate. For example:

Density = $\frac{mass}{volume}$ has units such as g/cm³ (grams per cubic centimetre)

Speed = $\frac{distance}{time}$ has units such as m/s (metres per second) or km/h (kilometres per hour)

Focus

Example 1

Which is faster, a car travelling at 30 mph or a bus travelling at 45 km/h?

÷5 (5 miles = 8 km) ÷5 1 mile = 1.6 km ×30 (30 miles = 48 km) ×30 30 mph = 48 km/h	Start by using the fact that 5 miles = 8 kilometres Divide each value by 5 to find out how many kilometres are equal to 1 mile. Find out how many kilometres are equal to 30 miles. So you know 30 mph is equal to 48 km/h. You may have spotted that 30 = 5 × 6 and just multiplied 8 km by 6
30 mph is faster than 45 km/h	48 km/h is greater than 45 km/h so 30 mph is faster than 45 km/h.

Example 2

a) Emily completes an 8 km race in 52 minutes and 6 seconds.

   Calculate Emily's average speed in metres per second. Give your answer to 2 decimal places.

b) Zach completes the same 8 km race. His average speed is 5.2 miles per hour.

   Convert Zach's speed to metres per second.

a) 8 × 1000 = 8000 8 km = 8000 metres	There are 1000 metres in a kilometre, so to convert kilometres to metres you multiply by 1000
52 × 60 = 3120 52 minutes = 3120 seconds	There are 60 seconds in a minute, so to convert minutes to seconds you multiply by 60
3120 + 6 = 3126 seconds	You then need to add the 6 seconds to find the total time.
speed = $\frac{distance}{time}$ speed = $\frac{8000}{3126}$ = 2.56 m/s	Substitute the values into the formula to work out her average speed in metres per second.

b) 1 mile = 1.6 km

$\times 1.6 \left\langle \begin{array}{l} 5.2\,\text{mph} \\ 8.32\,\text{km/h} \end{array} \right.$

$\times 1000 \left\langle \begin{array}{ll} 8.32\,\text{km} & 1\,\text{hour} \\ 8320\,\text{metres} & 1\,\text{hour} \\ 138.666...\,\text{metres} & 1\,\text{minute} \\ 2.311...\,\text{metres} & 1\,\text{second} \end{array} \right. \begin{array}{l} \\ \div 60 \\ \div 60 \\ \div 60 \end{array}$
$\div 60$
$\div 60$

2.31 m/s

As 5 miles = 8 kilometres, you can use the fact that 1 mile = 1.6 km to convert the speed to km/h.

Then change km to m.
Then change hours to minutes.
Then change minutes to seconds.
Give your answer to a sensible degree of accuracy.

Fluency

1. A person cycles round a 400-metre track in 45 seconds.
   a) Write 400 metres in kilometres.
   b) Convert 45 seconds to hours.
   c) Calculate the cyclist's speed in km/h.

2. A runner completes an 800-metre race in 2 minutes and 47 seconds.
   What is their average speed in m/s? Give your answer to 1 decimal place.

3. The maximum speed of a train is 240 km/h.
   Convert this speed to m/s, giving your answer to 3 significant figures.

4. Rhys drives a car at a speed of 90 km/h. The speed limit for the road is 60 mph.
   Is Rhys driving within the speed limit?

5. A tortoise travels 0.75 metres in 5 seconds. A hare travels at 50 km/h.
   How much further does the hare travel in one hour than the tortoise?

6. An athlete's maximum speed is 10.4 m/s.
   Convert this speed to miles per hour.

7. Find the pressure exerted by a force of 300 Newtons on an area of 75 cm². Give your answer in N/m²

   Use the formula pressure = $\dfrac{\text{force}}{\text{area}}$

8. Look at the diagram of the pond shown on the right.
   a) What is the volume of the pond? Give your answer in litres.

   The empty pond is filled at a constant rate of 400 litres per minute.

   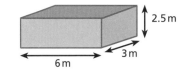
   2.5 m
   3 m
   6 m

   b) How long does it take to fill the pond completely with water? Give your answer in hours.

9. A piece of wood has a volume of 2500 cm³ and a density of 0.78 g/cm³
   Work out the mass of the wood, giving your answer to the nearest kilogram.

   Rearrange the formula
   density = $\dfrac{\text{mass}}{\text{volume}}$

Further

1. The mass of a gold sphere is 18.4 grams. The volume of the sphere is 0.95 cm³
   Work out the density of the gold sphere in kg/m³, giving your answer to 1 decimal place.   (3 marks)

2. The density of silver is 10.5 g/cm³. 0.9 m³ of bronze has a mass of 7920 kg.
   Which has the greater density, silver or bronze?   (3 marks)

3. A race is 30 km in length. The average speed for the winner is 12.5 mph. The second person to complete the race finished 1 minute and 13 seconds after the winner.

   What was the average speed of the person who came second?
   Give your answer in m/s to 2 decimal places.   (4 marks)

3.3 Direct and inverse proportion

Foundations

A car travels at a constant speed of 60 mph.

a) How long does it take the car to travel 30 miles?

b) If the speed of the car is increased, would the time taken to travel 30 miles increase or decrease?

Facts

Two quantities are in **direct proportion** when, as one increases, the other increases at the same rate.

For example, one mango costs 40 pence. When you increase the number of mangoes, the cost increases at the same rate, i.e. twice as many mangoes would mean double the cost.

	Number of mangoes	Cost (pence)	
× 2	1	40	× 2
	2	80	

Two quantities are in **inverse proportion** when, as one increases, the other decreases at the same rate. For example, suppose it takes one person 10 minutes to complete a task.

When you increase the number of people, the time taken decreases at the same rate, i.e. twice as many people would mean half the time.

This assumes that both people are working at the same rate.

	People	Number of minutes	
× 2	1	10	÷ 2
	2	5	

Focus

Example 1

Lida pays £12 for 5 litres of oil.

a) How much does 16 litres of oil cost?   **b)** How many litres of oil can Lida buy with £30?

a) 12 ÷ 5 = 2.4 1 litre of oil costs £2.40	Divide £12 by 5 to work out the cost of 1 litre of oil.
£2.40 × 16 = £38.40 16 litres of oil costs £38.40	Now you can work out the cost of 16 litres by multiplying 16 by £2.40 There are other ways of working this out. For example, you could work out how many times greater 16 litres is than 5 litres.
b) £30 ÷ £12 = 2.5	One way is to work out how many times greater £30 is than £12
5 × 2.5 = 12.5 £30 buys 12.5 litres of oil	If the price paid is 2.5 times greater, you can buy 2.5 times as much oil.

You could use a proportion diagram to solve this problem.

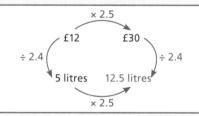

You could also use the fact that 1 litre costs £2.40 and work out £30 ÷ £2.40 = 12.5

Example 2

In a factory, two machines can fill 800 bottles in 3 hours. Working at the same rate, how long will it take six machines to fill 800 bottles?

6 ÷ 2 = 3	There are three times as many machines.
3 hours ÷ 3 = 1 hour	More machines working at the same rate means it will take less time, so you divide 3 hours by 3

Fluency

1 Five identical books cost £16

   a) Work out the cost of seven of the books.

   b) If seven of the books weigh 2.8 kg, how much do nine of the books weigh?

2 A recipe states that you need 3 eggs to make 15 cupcakes.

   a) How many eggs would be needed to make 50 cupcakes?

   To make 15 cupcakes, you need 150 grams of flour. Millie has 750 grams of flour and plenty of other ingredients.

   b) How many cupcakes can Millie make?

   Seth has 12 eggs and 650 grams of flour and plenty of other ingredients.

   c) Work out the greatest number of cupcakes Seth can make.

3 Five people construct a building in 20 days. Assuming that all the people work at the same rate, how long would it take to construct the building with:

   a) one person working?   **b)** ten people working?

4 The cost of cleaning an office building is directly proportional to the time spent cleaning it. If it takes 3 hours to clean a building, it costs £36.75

   a) How much would it cost for a building that takes 2 hours to clean?

   b) How many hours would it take to clean a building if the cost is £98?

5 Using 3 pumps, a swimming pool can be emptied in 60 minutes.

   a) How long will it take to empty the swimming pool using: **i)** 1 pump?   **ii)** 12 pumps?

   b) The formula connecting the number of pumps (p) and the time taken (T) is $T = \frac{180}{p}$

   Use this formula to work out the time it takes to empty the pool using: **i)** 5 pumps   **ii)** 8 pumps

6 g is inversely proportional to h.
   Complete the table.

g	6		5	4
h	5	15		

Further

1 A three-litre bottle of orange juice costs £3.15
   A 750 ml bottle of orange juice costs 78 pence.

   Is the cost of orange juice directly proportional to the amount of orange juice in the bottle? Show your working.   (3 marks)

2 Six workers can pack 300 boxes in 1 hour and 20 minutes.

   a) Assuming that the workers pack at the same rate, how long would it take five workers to pack the same number of boxes? Give your answer in hours and minutes.   (2 marks)

   b) How many workers would be needed to pack 300 boxes in a quarter of the time taken by six?   (2 marks)

3 Decide whether the relationships are directly proportional, inversely proportional or neither.

   a) Given a fixed hourly rate, the more hours you work, the more money you are paid.   (1 mark)

   b) The fewer students in a class, the more work they have to complete.   (1 mark)

   c) As the speed of a van increases, the time it takes to travel a distance decreases.   (1 mark)

4 Bobbie takes 3 hours to build a wall. Abdullah takes 2 hours to build a wall of the same size.
   If they work together, how long will it take them to build one wall of this size? Give your answer in hours and minutes.   (3 marks)

3.4 Rates of change

White Rose Maths

Foundations

1. £1 can buy €1.20

   a) How many euros (€) can be bought with £60? b) How many pounds (£) can be bought with €60 euros?

2. A straight line goes through the points (0, 0) and (5, 15). Work out the gradient of the line.

Facts

The **rate of change** is a comparison between two quantities.

Rates are often expressed in the form 'one unit per another unit'. For example, speed can be given as a rate of 'miles per hour', a machine might produce components measured in 'amount per minute', etc.

On a graph, the rate of change is the **gradient** (the steepness) of a line.

Rates are not always constant and can change over time.

Focus

Example
Water flows into three tanks labelled A, B and C.

a) It takes $2\frac{1}{2}$ minutes to fill tank A with 15 litres of water. Calculate the rate, in litres per minute, at which tank A is filling with water.

b) The capacity of tank A is 900 litres. How long will it take to completely fill the tank, assuming a constant rate of flow? Give your answer in hours and minutes.

The graph shows how the volumes of water in tanks B and C change over time.

c) How do you know the tanks are filling at a constant rate?

d) Work out the rate of flow for tanks B and C.

a)	Rate = 15 ÷ 2.5 = 6 litres per minute	Divide the amount of water in the tank by the time taken to fill it. $2\frac{1}{2}$ = 2.5
b)	900 ÷ 6 = 150	A rate of 6 litres/minute means that 6 litres flow into the tank each minute. So you need to work out how many lots of 6 litres there are in 900 litres.
	150 minutes = 2 hours and 30 minutes	There are 60 minutes in an hour.
c)	The lines both have a constant gradient, therefore the depth of water in the tanks will increase at a constant rate.	As the lines are straight and go through the origin, the volume of water is directly proportional to the time.
d)		The rate of flow is the gradient of the line. Use (0, 0) and a point with coordinates that you can easily read to find the rate. The point (3, 30) can be used for B and (4, 15) for C.
	Rate of flow for B = $\frac{30 \text{ litres}}{3 \text{ minutes}}$ = 10 litres/min Rate of flow for C = $\frac{15 \text{ litres}}{4 \text{ minutes}}$ = 3.75 litres/min	Divide the number of litres by the time taken. The gradient of the graph is the speed at which the tank is filling. Line B has a steeper gradient than line C, so you know tank B is filling at a faster rate.

Fluency

1 Here is a graph showing the flow of water into a tank.

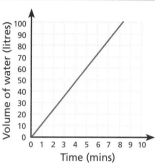

   a) Find the rate of flow in litres per minute.

   b) How much water will flow into the tank in 30 minutes?

   c) The capacity of a tank is 1500 litres. How long will it take
   to completely fill the tank using the rate of flow from part a)?

2 A machine can make 480 bottles an hour.

   a) What is the rate of bottles made per minute?

   b) At the same rate, how many bottles can the machine make in a week?

3 The graph shows the cost of hiring a plumber. The plumber charges a
call-out fee, then a fixed charge per hour.

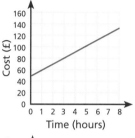

   a) What is the plumber's fixed charge?

   b) What is the plumber's hourly rate?

4 The two lines on the graph show the water flow out of two tanks, A and B.

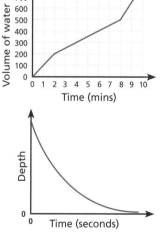

   a) Which tank has water flowing out at the faster rate? Explain how you know.

   b) Work out the rate of change for each tank.

   c) What does the gradient of each line represent?

Further

1 The graph shows a tank being filled at different rates.

   a) Between which times was the rate of flow the fastest?   (1 mark)

   b) Work out the rate at which the tank was being filled:

      i)   in the first 2 minutes   (1 mark)

      ii) between 2 and 8 minutes   (1 mark)

      iii) between 8 and 10 minutes   (1 mark)

   c) Work out the average rate at which the tank was being filled
   over the 10-minute period.   (2 marks)

2 Water is being emptied out of a bath. The graph shows the
depth of water in the bath over time.

   Does the water empty out at a constant rate?
   Explain how you know.   (2 marks)

3 Water is poured at a constant rate into these three containers. Match each container to the graph
which shows how the depth of water changes with time.   (3 marks)

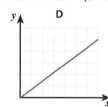
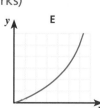
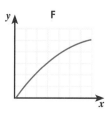

3.5 Compound interest

Foundations

1 What multiplier would be used to:

    a) increase by 35%?   **b)** increase by 8%?   **c)** decrease by 15%?   **d)** increase by 2.8%?

2 **a)** Increase £5600 by 2.7%   **b)** Decrease £20 000 by 8%

Facts

Repeated percentage change is when an amount is changed by a percentage more than once.

Interest is a percentage earned when you deposit money or a percentage fee paid when borrowing money. For **simple interest**, the same amount is added every year, but for **compound interest** the interest is added on every year and earns interest itself.

Paying money into a bank account is known as a **deposit** or an **investment**.

Per annum means for each year.

Depreciate means to decrease in value.

Focus

Example 1

Lily invests £4500 in a savings account earning 3.5% compound interest per annum.

How much money will she have in her account after 3 years?

100% + 3.5% = 103.5% = 1.035	Start by working out the decimal multiplier. The multiplier for a 3.5% increase is 1.035
After 1 year: £4500 × 1.035 = £4657.50 After 2 years: £4657.50 × 1.035 = £4820.5125 After 3 years: £4820.5125 × 1.035 = £4989.230 438	Work out the total value of Lily's savings after each year for 3 years. Multiply the total amount in the account at the end of each year by 1.035 This is the same as working out £4500 × 1.035^3
= £4989.23	Round your answer to 2 decimal places for money.

Example 2

A ball is dropped from a height of 3.2 metres. After each bounce, it loses 25% of its height.

What height will it reach on its fourth bounce?

100% − 25% = 75% = 0.75	Start by working out the decimal multiplier. The multiplier for a 25% decrease is 0.75
After 1 bounce: 3.2 × 0.75 = 2.4 m After 2 bounces: 2.4 × 0.75 = 1.8 m After 3 bounces: 1.8 × 0.75 = 1.35 m After 4 bounces: 1.35 × 0.75 = 1.0125 m	Work out the height of the ball after each bounce for the four bounces. Multiply the height at the end of the previous bounce by 0.75 This is the same as working out 3.2 × 0.75^4
3.2 × 0.75^4 = 1.0125 metres	

Fluency

1. Which calculation represents the total amount of money after £2000 is invested at 3% compound interest per annum for 5 years?

   2000×1.3^5 2000×1.05^3 2000×1.03^5

2. Six years ago, Mario bought a car for £25 000. The value of the car has depreciated by 9% per year.

   Find the current value of Mario's car.

3. The number of bacteria cells in a Petri dish increases by 12% each hour.

   If there were originally 250 cells, how many cells are there after 4 hours?

4. In a sale, items are reduced by 15%. A week later, items are reduced by a further 20%

   Work out the price of a coat that cost £85 before the sale.

5. Chloe wants to invest £4000 for 9 years.

Bank 1
1.8% compound interest per annum

Bank 2
4% interest for the first year 1% compound interest for additional years

   Which bank will give Chloe the most interest after 9 years?

6. Sven deposits £200 in a savings account that pays compound interest per annum. To find the value of his investment after 8 years, Sven uses the formula $V = 200 \times 1.056^8$

   What is the annual rate of interest that Sven earns?

7. The world's population is 7.9 billion. The population of the world is growing at a rate of 1.05% each year.

   Estimate the population of the world 10 years from now.

Further

1. Hassan invests £9600 in a savings account that pays 2.7% compound interest per annum.

   After n years, Hassan has £11 880.50 in his account.

   Work out the value of n. (2 marks)

2. Petra invests £3500 at y% compound interest per annum.

   After 5 years, she has £4683.79 in her account.

   Work out the value of y. (3 marks)

3. Faith invests £7000 at 4% compound interest per annum.

   Jackson invests £9000 at 1.5% compound interest per annum.

   After how many years will Faith's investment exceed Jackson's? (3 marks)

4. What is the overall percentage change if an amount is increased by 10% a total of four times?

5. Leo invests £m into a savings account paying x% compound interest per annum.

   After 5 years, Leo's investment is worth £5120.22

   After 6 years, Leo's investment is worth £5186.78

   Work out the values of m and x. (3 marks)

4F1 Angles

Facts

An **angle** is a measure of turn.

Angles in a **full turn** add up to 360°

Adjacent angles on a **straight line** add up to 180°

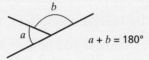

Vertically opposite angles are equal.

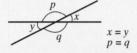

Angles in a **triangle** add up to 180°

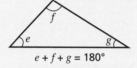

Angles in a **quadrilateral** add up to 360°

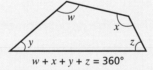

The sum of the **interior** angles of a polygon with n sides is $(n - 2) \times 180°$

The sum of the **exterior** angles of any polygon is 360°

Angles can be described using **three-letter** notation.

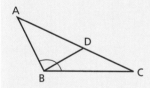

Angle ABC is marked
with an arc

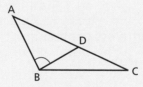

Angle ABD is marked
with an arc

Equal angles are shown by the same arcs. Equal sides are
shown by the same number of hatch marks. The diagram
shows that opposite angles of a parallelogram are equal
in size, and the opposite sides are equal in length.

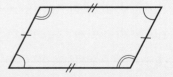

Base angles (the angles between the equal sides and the
other side) in an **isosceles triangle** are equal.

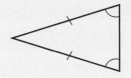

Practice

The diagrams below are not drawn accurately. This instruction in an exam tells you to work out or calculate, rather than measure, any angles you need to know.

1. Work out the sizes of the angles marked with letters.

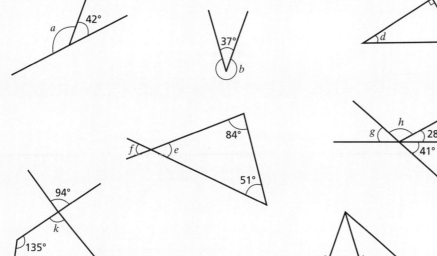
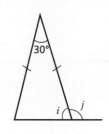

2. One angle in an isosceles triangle is 50°

   What are the possibilities for the other two angles?

3. Work out the sum of the interior angles in an octagon.

4. The interior angles of a regular polygon are 170°

   a) Work out the size of each exterior angle of the polygon.

   b) How many sides does the polygon have?

5. The diagram shows a square ABDE and equilateral triangle BCD.

   Work out the size of angle:

   a) ADB

   b) ABC

   c) ADC

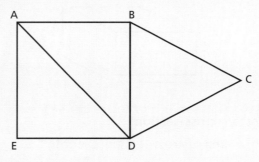

6. PQR is a straight line.

   Work out the size of angle QSR.

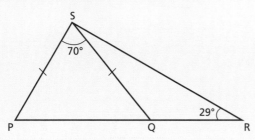

Facts

Area measures the space inside a 2-D shape. Area is measured in squared units such as cm², mm² and m².
Here are the formulae for working out A, the area of some basic shapes.

Rectangle

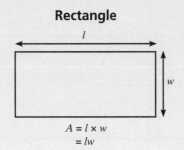

$$A = l \times w$$
$$= lw$$

Parallelogram

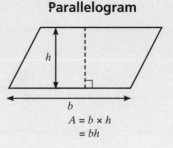

$$A = b \times h$$
$$= bh$$

Triangle

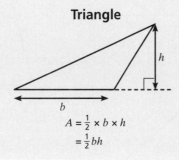

$$A = \tfrac{1}{2} \times b \times h$$
$$= \tfrac{1}{2}bh$$

Trapezium

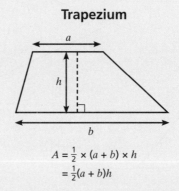

$$A = \tfrac{1}{2} \times (a + b) \times h$$
$$= \tfrac{1}{2}(a + b)h$$

Notice that h stands for the **perpendicular height**, which must be at right angles to the base of the shape.

The area, A, of a **circle** is given by the formula $A = \pi r^2$, where r is the radius of the circle.

> Be careful not to confuse this with $C = \pi d$, which gives the circumference of a circle of diameter d. This can also be written as $C = 2\pi r$, giving the circumference in terms of a circle's radius r.

Volume measures the space occupied by a 3-D shape. Volume is measured in cubic units such as cm³, mm³ and m³.

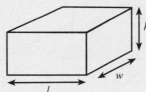

Volume of a cuboid
$$= l \times w \times h$$
$$= lwh$$

A **prism** has a constant **cross-section**.

Volume of a prism = area of cross-section × length

The volume, V, of a **cylinder** of radius r and height h is given by the formula $V = \pi r^2 h$

Practice

1 Find the areas of the shapes.

a)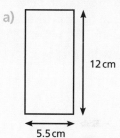
12 cm
5.5 cm

b)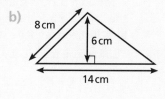
8 cm
6 cm
14 cm

c)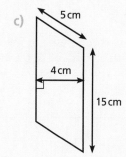
5 cm
4 cm
15 cm

d)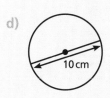
10 cm

e)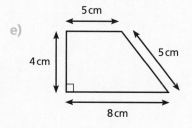
5 cm
4 cm
5 cm
8 cm

2 The base of a triangle is 7 cm long.

The area of the triangle is 42 cm²

Work out the height of the triangle.

3 A cuboid has a square base with sides 3 m.

The height of the cuboid is 12 m.

Work out the volume of the cuboid.

4 A trapezium with an area of 60 cm² has parallel sides of length 7 cm and 8 cm.

Work out the perpendicular height of the trapezium.

5 Find the volume of a cube with sides 6 cm.

6 A square has perimeter 28 cm.

Find the area of the square.

7 The base of a cylinder has radius 4 cm.

The height of the cylinder is 12 cm.

Find the volume of the cylinder, giving your answer in terms of π

8 The area of the parallelogram is three times the area of the triangle.

Work out the height of the parallelogram.

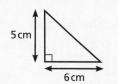
5 cm
6 cm

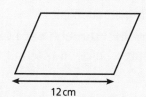
12 cm

9 How many cubes with side length 2 cm will fit inside a cuboid of length 8 cm, width 6 cm and height 4 cm?

10 The diagram shows a triangular prism.

Work out the volume of the triangular prism.

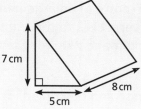
7 cm
8 cm
5 cm

Facts

A **reflection** is a transformation that produces the image of a shape in a mirror line. A reflected image is always congruent to the original. This means that it is exactly the same size and shape as the object. Each point of the image is the same perpendicular distance from the mirror line as the corresponding point on the object.	A **rotation** turns a shape around a fixed point, called the centre of rotation. Rotations can be clockwise or anticlockwise and are usually through 90°, 180° or 270° You can use tracing paper to help with rotations.
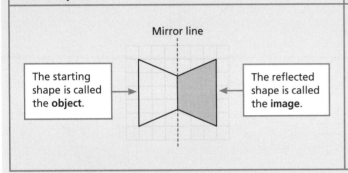	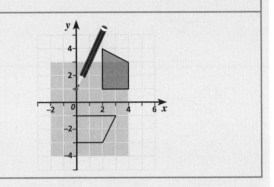

A **translation** is a transformation that moves a shape vertically, horizontally or both.

Translations can be described using **vector** notation.

The number at the top of the vector represents a move to the right (if positive) or to the left (if negative).

The number on the bottom of the vector represents a move up (if positive) or down (if negative).

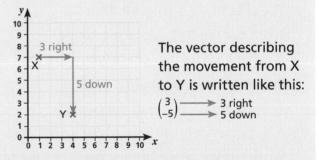

The vector describing the movement from X to Y is written like this:

$$\binom{3}{-5} \longrightarrow \begin{array}{l}\text{3 right}\\\text{5 down}\end{array}$$

Enlargement is a transformation that makes a shape bigger or smaller. The **scale factor** tells you how much to enlarge the shape by and the **centre of enlargement** tells you where to draw the enlargement.

A scale factor greater than 1 will result in the shape getting bigger.

A scale factor between 0 and 1 will result in the shape getting smaller.

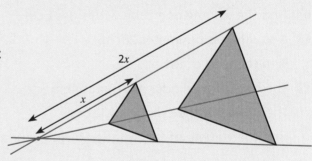

Drawing ray lines through each vertex on the original shape and the corresponding vertex on the enlarged shape helps you to find the centre of enlargement, which is where the rays meet.

You can also enlarge a shape by counting squares on a grid. The larger triangle is an enlargement of the smaller triangle by scale factor 2. Each vertex is twice as far from the centre of enlargement (marked with a cross). For example, the bottom left vertex is 2 to the right and 1 up for the smaller triangle and 4 to the right and 2 up for the larger triangle.

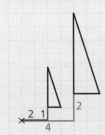

You need to be able to recognise and describe all four types of transformation as well as perform them.

Practice

You can use tracing paper to help with reflections and rotations.

1 a) Reflect the shape in the *x*-axis.

 b) Reflect the shape in the *y*-axis.

 c) Reflect the shape in the line *x* = 3

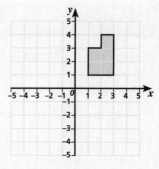

2 a) Rotate the shape 90° clockwise about (0, 0)

 b) Rotate the shape 180° about (1, 2)

 c) Rotate the shape 90° anticlockwise about (0, 0)

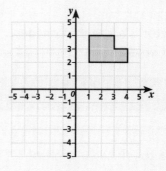

3 a) Translate the shape by the vector $\begin{pmatrix} 3 \\ 2 \end{pmatrix}$

 b) Translate the shape by the vector $\begin{pmatrix} 2 \\ -3 \end{pmatrix}$

 c) Translate the shape by the vector $\begin{pmatrix} -1 \\ -4 \end{pmatrix}$

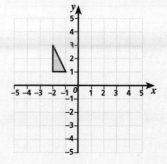

4 Enlarge the shape by scale factor 3, centre of enlargement A.

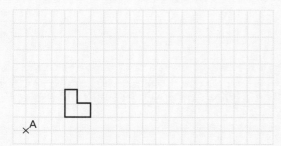

Foundations

Accurately draw angles measuring: **a)** 48°   **b)** 162°   **c)** 245°

Facts

Constructions are accurate drawings made using a ruler and a pair of compasses.
It is important that you do not rub out your construction lines
once you have completed the construction.

A **bisector** is a line that divides something into two equal parts.

An **angle bisector** is a line that divides
an angle into two equal parts.

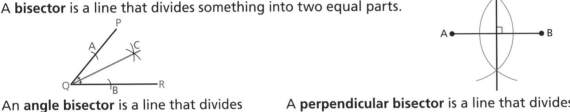

A **perpendicular bisector** is a line that divides a line segment
into two equal parts and is perpendicular to the original line.

Focus

Example 1

Using a protractor, draw an angle of 60°. Using a pair of compasses and a ruler, construct its angle bisector.

	Start by drawing an angle of 60°. Make the arms of the angle about 6 cm long.
	Use a pair of compasses to draw an arc of radius about 4 cm from the vertex of the angle that cuts both arms of the angle. Label these points of intersection A and B.
	Next, draw two more equal length arcs from A and B. Make sure you draw them long enough so that they meet.
	Draw a straight line from the vertex of the angle through the point of intersection of the two arcs.
	Check that both angles are 30°

Example 2

Draw a line segment of 9cm. Construct its perpendicular bisector.

9 cm A——————B	Draw a 9cm line segment.
	Draw arcs with radius of equal length from both ends of the line segment. The radius of the arcs must be more than half the length of the line.
	Join the intersections of the arcs using a ruler.
	Check that each line segment measures 4.5cm.

Fluency

1. Use a ruler and a pair of compasses to construct these triangles.

   a) ABC with AB = 8cm, BC = 7cm and AC = 4cm

   b) PQR with PQ = 4cm, QR = 5cm and PR = 6cm

2. Copy the three angles shown. Construct the angle bisector of each angle.

3. Draw an angle of 80° and construct its bisector.

4. Draw a line segment measuring 8cm and construct its perpendicular bisector.

5. Draw a line segment of 10cm and construct its perpendicular bisector.

Further

1. Using a ruler and a pair of compasses, construct an equilateral triangle with sides 7cm.   (3 marks)

You need to make copies of the diagrams for Further questions 2, 3 and 4

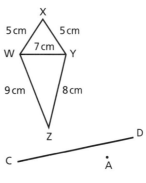

2. Use a ruler and a pair of compasses to construct the quadrilateral WXYZ.   (3 marks)

3. Use a ruler and a pair of compasses to construct the perpendicular from point A to the line CD.   (3 marks)

Start by constructing two points on CD equidistant from A.

4. Use a ruler and a pair of compasses to construct the perpendicular to AB through the point P.   (3 marks)

Start by constructing two points on AB equidistant from P.

5. Use a ruler and a pair of compasses to construct a 30° angle.   (3 marks)

Foundations

1. Draw an angle of 70° and construct its angle bisector.
2. Draw a line segment of 7 cm and construct its perpendicular bisector.

Facts

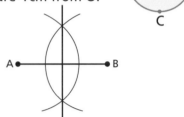

A **locus** (plural **loci**) is a set of points that all have a particular property.
In the circle, OA = OB = OC = 4 cm. The circle is the **locus** of the points that are 4 cm from O.

Another example is the locus of all points **equidistant** from two other
points, A and B. This means all the points that are the same distance
from A as they are from B. This would be the perpendicular bisector of
the line segment joining A and B. See unit 4.1 for how to construct this.

Focus

Example 1

ABCD is a square of side length 7 cm. O is at the centre of the square.

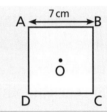

a) Draw the locus of all points 3 cm from O.

b) Shade the locus of all points inside the square that are more than 3 cm from O.

a) 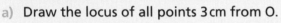	All the points that are exactly 3 cm from O form a circle, centre O with radius 3 cm.
b) 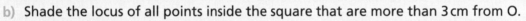	The points inside the circle are less than 3 cm from O. So you need to shade the region outside the circle, but within the square.

Example 2

ABCD is a square of side length 8 cm.

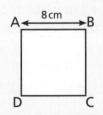

a) Draw the locus of all points inside the square and exactly 3 cm from AD.

b) Draw the locus of all points inside the square and 4 cm from D.

c) Shade the region of all points inside the square, less than 3 cm from AD
   and less than 4 cm from D.

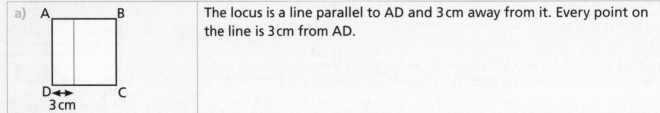

a)	The locus is a line parallel to AD and 3 cm away from it. Every point on the line is 3 cm from AD.

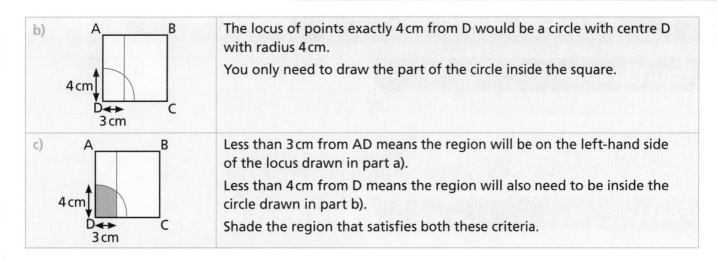

b)	The locus of points exactly 4 cm from D would be a circle with centre D with radius 4 cm.
	You only need to draw the part of the circle inside the square.
c)	Less than 3 cm from AD means the region will be on the left-hand side of the locus drawn in part a).
	Less than 4 cm from D means the region will also need to be inside the circle drawn in part b).
	Shade the region that satisfies both these criteria.

Fluency

① Mark a point O on a blank page. Draw the locus of all points exactly 5 cm from O.

② Construct the locus of points that are between 5 cm and 7 cm from a point X.

③ Draw a line segment AB, 7 cm long.

   a) Construct the locus of all points 3 cm from A.

   b) Construct the locus of all points 5 cm from B.

   c) Identify the points that are both 3 cm from A and 5 cm from B.

④ Construct the locus of all points 3 cm from a copy of the line segment XY.

X ————————————— Y

⑤ A supermarket is going to be built. It must be no more than 8 km from village A and no more than 6 km from village B. The diagram shows the location of village A and village B. 1 cm represents 2 km.

On a copy of the diagram, shade the region where the supermarket can be built.

A×

B
×

Further

Make two copies of this diagram to answer the Further questions.

① ABCD is a scale drawing of a garden. The scale is 1 cm = 2 m

A tree is to be planted. It must be more than 4 m from the pond (P).

Shade the region where the tree can be planted.   (2 marks)

② ABCD is a scale drawing of a garden. The scale is 1 cm = 2 m

A tree is to be planted. It must be more than 4 m from the pond (P) **and** less than 3 m from the fence AB.

On the same diagram you used for question 1, shade the region where the tree can be planted.   (3 marks)

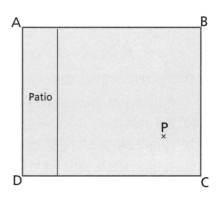

③ ABCD is a scale drawing of a garden. The scale is 1 cm = 2 m

A tree is to be planted. It must be closer to AB than to BC **and** it must be more than 2 m from the patio.

Shade the region where the tree can be planted.   (3 marks)

Foundations

Work out the sizes of the angles marked with letters.

a)

b)

c)

d)

e)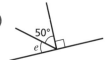

Facts

A line through a pair of parallel lines is called a **transversal**.

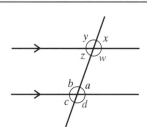	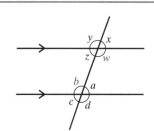	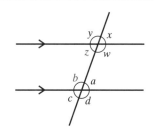
Angles w and d are called **corresponding** angles. They are to the right of the transversal and both below the parallel lines – they are in corresponding positions.	Angles w and b are called **alternate** angles. They are between the parallel lines but on alternate sides of the transversal.	Angles z and b are called **co-interior** angles. They are on the same side of the transversal and between the parallel lines.
Corresponding angles in parallel lines are equal, so $w = d$, $y = b$, $x = a$ and $z = c$	Alternate angles in parallel lines are equal, so $b = w$ and $z = a$	Co-interior angles add up to 180°, so $z + b = 180°$ and $a + w = 180°$

Focus

Example 1

Find the value of each labelled angle. Give reasons for your answers.

a)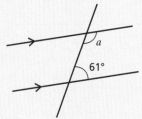

b)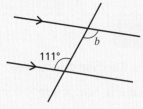

c)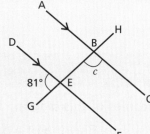

a) $a = 180° - 61° = 119°$	Angle a and the 61° angle are co-interior.
Co-interior angles add up to 180°	Give your reasons, using precise mathematical language.
b) $b = 111°$	Angle b and the 111° angle are alternate.
Alternate angles are equal.	
c) Angle DEB = 180° − 81° = 99°	Alternatively:
Angles on a straight line add up to 180°	Angle BEF = 81° (vertically opposite angles are equal)
Angle c = 99°	$c = 180° − 81° = 99°$ (co-interior angles add up to 180°)
Alternate angles are equal.	

Example 2

Work out the values of x and y.

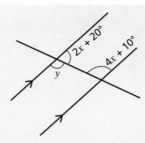

$2x + 20° + 4x + 10° = 180°$	$2x + 20°$ and $4x + 10°$ are co-interior angles and add up to $180°$ Set up an equation using this fact.
$6x + 30° = 180°$ $6x = 150°$ $x = 25°$	Simplify and solve the equation.
$2x + 20° + y = 180°$	The y angle and the $2x + 20°$ angle are adjacent angles on a straight line. They add up to $180°$
$50° + 20° + y = 180°$	You know $x = 25°$, so $2x = 50°$
$70° + y = 180°$	Simplify and solve the equation.
$y = 110°$	

Fluency

1. Work out the sizes of the unknown angles, giving reasons for your answers.

a)

b)

c)

d)

2. Work out the size of the angle marked x.

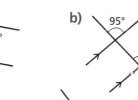

3. Work out the size of each of the unknown angles, giving reasons.

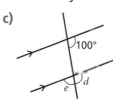

4. ABCD is a parallelogram. ADE is a straight line.

   Find the size of angle ECD. Give reasons for
   each stage in your working.

5. Work out the size of the angle marked x. Give reasons for each stage in your working.

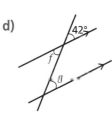

Further

1. Work out the values of x and y. (3 marks)

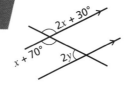

2. Find the size of angle CFG.
   Give reasons for each stage in your working. (2 marks)

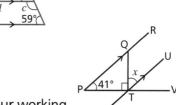

3. WXYZ is a parallelogram.

   Calculate the size of angle WOX. (3 marks)

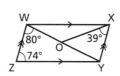

4. Are line segments AB and CD parallel? Give a reason for your answer. (2 marks)

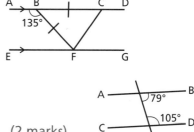

4.4 Fractional enlargement

Foundations

Draw a rectangle measuring 2 cm by 3 cm.

Enlarge the rectangle by scale factor 4

Facts

Enlargement is a transformation that makes a shape bigger or smaller.

To enlarge a shape, you will be given a **scale factor** and a **centre of enlargement**. The scale factor will tell you how much to enlarge the shape by and the centre of enlargement means that the enlarged shape must be drawn in a specific place.

A scale factor greater than 1 will result in the shape getting bigger. A scale factor between 0 and 1 will result in the shape getting smaller.

Drawing ray lines through each vertex on the original shape and the corresponding vertex on the enlarged shape can help you to find the centre of enlargement.

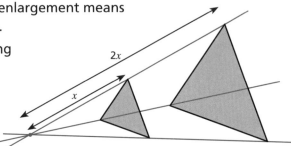

Focus

Example

Enlarge shape A by scale factor $\frac{1}{2}$ using the given centre of enlargement.

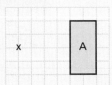

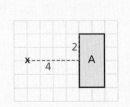	Count how far along and up it is from the centre of enlargement to one vertex of the shape. In this example, it is 4 to the right and 2 up. You can write this as the vector $\binom{4}{2}$ You need to enlarge this shape by scale factor $\frac{1}{2}$, so you can multiply this vector by $\frac{1}{2}$ as follows: $\binom{4}{2} \times \frac{1}{2} = \binom{2}{1}$
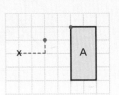	Use the vector $\binom{2}{1}$ from the centre of enlargement to work out where to draw the first vertex of the new shape.
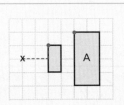	Repeat this for the other vertices in order to draw the enlarged shape. Because the scale factor is $\frac{1}{2}$, the new shape's dimensions are half the size of the original.

Fluency

1 Enlarge each shape by scale factor $\frac{1}{2}$ from the given centre of enlargement.

a)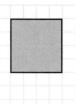

b)

2 Enlarge shape A by scale factor $\frac{1}{4}$, centre (0, 2)

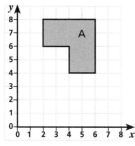

3 Enlarge shape B by scale factor $\frac{1}{3}$, centre (–1, 2)

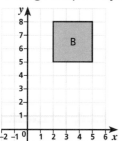

4 Describe fully the single transformation that maps shape P onto shape Q.

Further

1 Describe fully the single transformation that maps shape A onto shape B.   (3 marks)

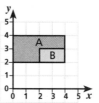

2 a) Enlarge triangle A by scale factor $\frac{1}{2}$, centre (2, 4)
Label your shape B.   (3 marks)

b) Compare the area of triangles A and B.   (1 mark)

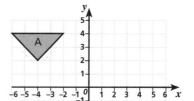

3 Enlarge shape A by scale factor $\frac{2}{3}$, centre (–3, 1)   (3 marks)

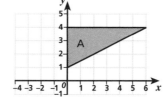

4.5 Bearings

Foundations

Measure the size of each of these angles.

a)   b)   c)   d)   e)

Facts

A bearing is an angle in degrees, measured clockwise from north. Bearings are usually written with three figures.

Bearing 060°

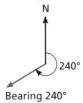
Bearing 240°

Bearing 330°

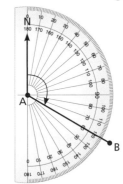

When asked to find the bearing of B from A, the 'from A' part tells you where to place your protractor.

Sometimes bearings questions are not drawn to scale, and you will need to use your knowledge of angles in parallel lines to solve problems. See unit 4.3

Focus

Example 1
a) Write down the bearing of A from O.
b) Work out the bearing of B from O.

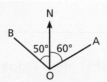

a) [diagram]	The bearing *from* O means you start from the north line at O and measure clockwise.
060°	From the diagram you can see the answer is 60° Remember to use three figures for bearings.
b) [diagram]	The bearing *from* O means you start from the north line at O and measure clockwise until you reach B.
360° − 50° = 310°	You can use facts about angles around a point to help.

Example 2
The accurate scale drawing shows two villages A and B.
Find the bearing of A from B.

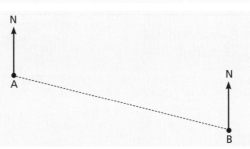

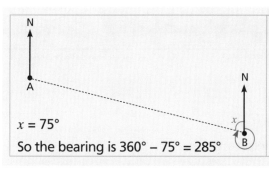

The bearing *from* B means you need to measure clockwise from the north line at B.

Since this is a reflex angle, it would be easier to measure the angle marked x and then subtract from 360°

Use a protractor to find the size of angle x.

$x = 75°$

So the bearing is 360° − 75° = 285°

Fluency

1 Look at the diagram shown right.

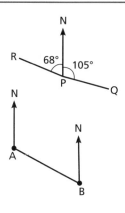

a) Write down the bearing of Q from P. b) Work out the bearing of R from P.

2 Look at the diagram shown right.

a) Measure the bearing of A from B. b) Find the bearing of B from A.

3 The accurate scale drawing shows the positions of school Y and school Z. A playground, P, is on a bearing of 055° from Y and on a bearing of 310° from Z.

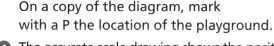

On a copy of the diagram, mark with a P the location of the playground.

4 The accurate scale drawing shows the positions of two points, P and Q. Point R is 5cm from P and on a bearing of 080°

a) Mark the position of R on a copy of the diagram.

b) Find the distance of Q to R.

c) Find the bearing of R from Q.

Further

1 The accurate scale drawing shows the positions of two towns, A and B. 1cm represents 2km.

a) Find the distance between towns A and B. (1 mark)

b) Measure the bearing of B from A. (1 mark)

c) A shopping centre is to be built 5km from town A and on a bearing of 200°

On a copy of the diagram, mark the position of the shopping centre. (2 marks)

d) Find the distance of the shopping centre from town B. (1 mark)

2 London is on a bearing of 160° from Leeds.

Find the bearing of Leeds from London. (2 marks)

4.6 Parts of a circle

Foundations

A circle has radius 5.5 cm.

a) Calculate the area of the circle, giving your answer to 2 decimal places.

b) Calculate the circumference of the circle, giving your answer in terms of π

Facts

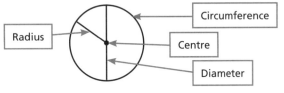

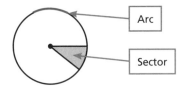

Circumference is a special name for the perimeter of a circle.

An **arc** is a part of the circumference of the circle. The **arc length** is a fraction of the circumference.

A **sector** is a part of a circle made by joining two points on the circumference to the centre of the circle. The **area of a sector** is a fraction of the total area of the circle.

You can use the formulae for the circumference and the area of circles, together with your knowledge of fractions, to find the length of an arc and the area of a sector.

In general, for angle θ:

$$\text{Arc length} = \frac{\theta}{360} \times \pi \times d \qquad \text{Area of sector} = \frac{\theta}{360} \times \pi \times r^2$$
$$= \frac{\theta}{360}\pi d \qquad\qquad\qquad = \frac{\theta}{360}\pi r^2$$

Focus

Example

a) Calculate the area of the sector AOB.

b) Calculate the length of arc AB.

c) Calculate the total perimeter of the sector AOB.

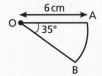

a) Area of sector = $\frac{\theta}{360} \times \pi \times r^2$	The area of the sector is a fraction of the total area of the circle.
Area = $\frac{35}{360} \times \pi \times 6^2$	The total area is $\pi \times 6^2$ Here, the fraction of the circle is $\frac{35}{360}$
Area = 10.9955... Area = 11.0 cm² (to 3 s.f.)	Calculate and round your answer sensibly.
b) Arc length = $\frac{\theta}{360} \times \pi \times d$	The length of the arc AB is a fraction of the total circumference.
Arc length = $\frac{35}{360} \times \pi \times 12$	The total circumference is $\pi \times 12$ Again, the fraction is $\frac{35}{360}$
Arc length = 3.66519... Arc length = 3.67 cm (to 3 s.f.)	Calculate and round your answer sensibly.
c) $P = AB + OA + OB$	The perimeter of AOB is made up of the arc length AB plus the straight lengths OA and OB.
$P = 3.67 + 6 + 6$	To find the perimeter, you add all these lengths together.
$P = 15.7$ cm (to 3 s.f.)	

Fluency

1 A circle has diameter 7 cm.

Calculate the area of the circle. Give your answer to 1 decimal place.

2 A circle has radius 3 cm.

Calculate the circumference of the circle. Give your answer in terms of π

3 A circle has area 80 cm²

Calculate the length of the radius of the circle. Round your answer to 1 decimal place.

4 An area is formed by a square PQRS and a semi-circle, as shown. The semi-circle has radius 5 cm.

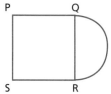

Calculate the area of the shape, giving your answer to 3 significant figures.

5 The diagram shows a sector, centre O.

a) Calculate the area of the sector, giving your answer in terms of π

b) Calculate the length of the arc AB, giving your answer to 2 decimal places.

c) Calculate the perimeter of AOB, giving your answer to 2 decimal places.

6 The diagram shows a sector OXY.

a) Calculate the area of the sector.

b) Calculate the perimeter of the sector.

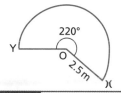

Further

1 A semi-circle has area 45 cm²

a) Calculate the radius of the semi-circle to 2 decimal places.   (2 marks)

b) Calculate the perimeter of the semi-circle to 2 decimal places.   (2 marks)

2 A circle is enclosed by a square with sides of length 6 cm, as shown.

Calculate the shaded area, giving your answer to 1 decimal place.   (2 marks)

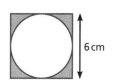

3 AOB is a sector of a circle with radius 12 cm.

The length of the arc AB is 4π cm.

a) Work out the size of angle x.   (2 marks)

b) Work out the area of the sector, giving your answer in terms of π (2 marks)

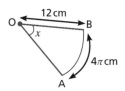

4 The diagram shows a semi-circle in a quadrant of another circle.

Work out the area of the shaded region. Give your answer in terms of π (3 marks)

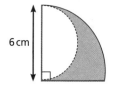

Foundations

Work out the area of each shape.

a)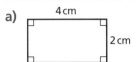

b)

c)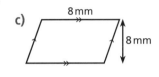

d)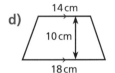

e)

f)

Facts

The **surface area** is the total area of all the faces of a 3-D shape. To work out the surface area, you need to find the area of all the faces individually and add them together. For example, a triangular prism is made up of three rectangular faces and two triangular faces.

For 3-D shapes with curved surfaces, you can find the surface area using formulae:

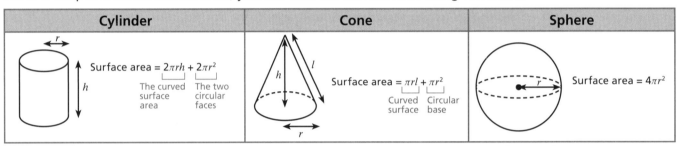

Volume is the amount of space a 3-D shape takes up. A prism is a 3-D shape with a uniform cross-section.

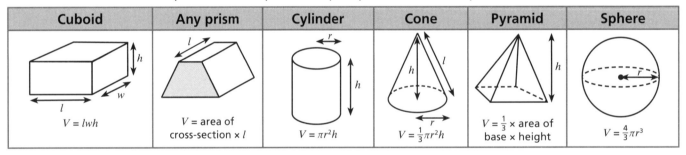

Focus

Example 1

A cuboid measures 6 cm by 4 cm by 3 cm.

Work out the cuboid's: a)   volume   b)   total surface area

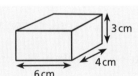

a)	Volume = 6 × 4 × 3	The volume of a cuboid = length × width × height
	Volume = 72 cm³	Remember the correct units.
b)	*net diagram: G (3cm); B, P, B, P with 3cm, 6cm, 3cm, 4cm; G*	You can use the net of a cuboid to help find the surface area. The net of a cuboid is made from six rectangles.
		Remember that the surface area is the total area of all of the faces.
	Blue faces: 3 × 4 = 12 cm² 12 × 2 = 24 cm² Pink faces: 6 × 4 = 24 cm² 24 × 2 = 48 cm² Green faces: 6 × 3 = 18 cm² 18 × 2 = 36 cm²	The faces come in pairs: the top and base, the front and back, and the left and right sides.
	24 + 48 + 36 = 108 cm²	Finally, add your answers and give the correct units.

Example 2

A wooden toy block is made from a cuboid and pyramid as shown.

Work out the volume of the shape.

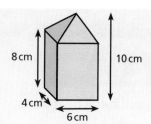

Volume of cuboid = 4 × 6 × 8 = 192 cm³	The cuboid measures 4 cm by 6 cm by 8 cm.
Volume of pyramid = $\frac{1}{3}$ × area of base × height Volume = $\frac{1}{3}$ × 4 × 6 × 2 = 16 cm³	The base of the pyramid is a rectangle measuring 4 cm by 6 cm. The height of the pyramid is 10 – 8 = 2 cm
Total volume = 192 + 16 = 208 cm³	Add the two volumes to find the total volume of the shape.

Fluency

1 For each cuboid, calculate the volume and the surface area.

a)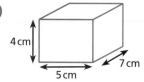

b)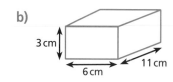

2 For each cylinder, calculate the volume and the surface area. Give your answers to 2 decimal places.

a)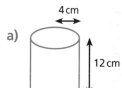

b)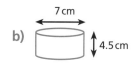

3 Work out the volume and surface area of each shape. In parts a) and b), give your answers in terms of π

a)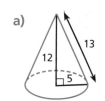

b)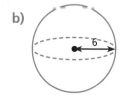

c)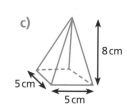

Further

1 The cuboid has volume 2520 cm³

Work out the length of the side marked x. (2 marks)

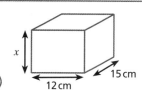

2 Work out the volume of the trapezoidal prism. (3 marks)

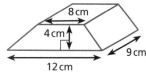

3 The diagram shows an empty fish tank.

The container is going to be filled using a jug with capacity 3 litres.

How many jugs of water will be needed to fill the tank? (3 marks)

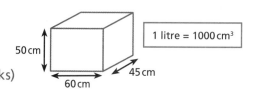

4 The total surface area of a cube is 294 cm²

Work out the volume of the cube. (3 marks)

5 The cube and the sphere have the same volume.

Work out the value of r, giving your answer to 3 significant figures. (3 marks)

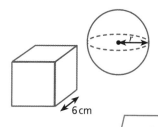

4.8 Congruent shapes

Foundations

Classify the triangles as isosceles, equilateral or scalene.

a)

b)

c)

d)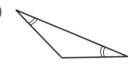

e)

Facts

Two shapes are **congruent** if they are exactly the same shape and size.

These three rectangles are congruent even though they are in different **orientations**.

There are four sets of conditions to determine if two triangles are congruent:

Side (SSS)	Side Angle Side (SAS)
  Three pairs of corresponding sides are equal.	 Two sides and the angle between them in one triangle are equal to the corresponding sides and angle of the other triangle.
Angle Angle Side (AAS)	**Right angle Hypotenuse Side (RHS)**
  Two angles and one side of a triangle are equal to the corresponding angles and side of the other triangle.	 One side and the hypotenuse in a right-angled triangle are equal to one side and the hypotenuse in the other right-angled triangle.

Focus

Example 1

Are shapes A and B congruent?
Explain your answer.

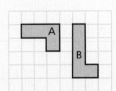

No, because shape B is longer than shape A.	If the lengths of all the sides or the sizes of all the angles in a pair of shapes are not the same, then the shapes are not congruent.

Example 2

Explain why the triangles in each given pair are congruent.

a)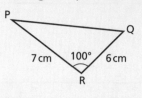

b)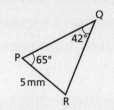

a)	Side AB = side QR (both 6 cm) Side BC = side PR (both 7 cm) Angle ABC = angle QRP (both 100°)	Write down which sides and angles are equal.
	So the Side Angle Side (SAS) condition shows they are congruent.	State which of the conditions you have used to show the congruence.
b)	Side AB = side PR (both 5 mm) Angle ABC = angle QPR (both 65°) Angle ACB = angle PQR (both 42°)	Write down which sides and angles are equal.
	So the Angle Angle Side (AAS) condition shows they are congruent.	State which of the conditions you have used to show the congruence.

Fluency

1 Here are some shapes.

a) Which shape is congruent to A?

b) Name a different pair of congruent shapes.

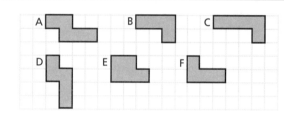

2 Triangles ABC and PQR are congruent.

a) Write down the length of QR.

b) Write down the length of PR.

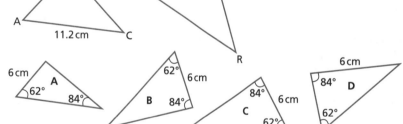

3 Four triangles A, B, C and D are shown.
Which two triangles are congruent?
How do you know?

4 Explain why each pair of triangles are congruent.

a)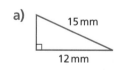

b)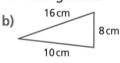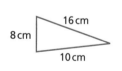

c)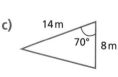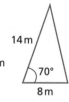

Further

1 Are the given pair of triangles congruent?
Explain your answer. (2 marks)

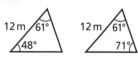

2 Identify a pair of congruent triangles from shapes A to D. Justify your answer. (2 marks)

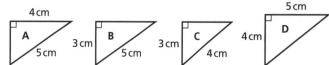

3 ABCD is a parallelogram.

Explain why triangles ABC
and ADC are congruent. (3 marks)

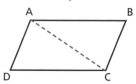

Foundations

a) $6 \times \text{.......} = 12$ b) $8 \times \text{.......} = 4$ c) $3 \times \text{.......} = 9$ d) $4 \times \text{.......} = 6$

Facts

Two triangles are similar if corresponding lengths are opposite equal angles:

 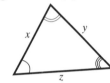

See more about similar shapes in unit 3.1

Here, the scale factor of enlargement is $\frac{x}{a}$ or $\frac{y}{b}$ or $\frac{z}{c}$. The ratios $x : a$, $y : b$ and $z : c$ are all equivalent.

To show that two triangles are similar, you have to show that **either** they have equal angles **or** that the corresponding sides are all in the same ratio.

Focus

Example 1
Triangles ABC and PQR are similar.

Calculate the lengths of AC and PR.

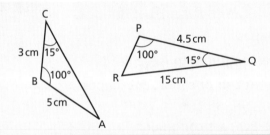

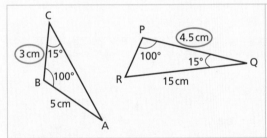	First you need to identify the sides which are corresponding. You can see that PQ and CB are corresponding sides, as they both lie between the 100° and 15° angles.
Scale factor = 4.5 ÷ 3 = 1.5	You can use these lengths to find the scale factor.
To find AC: AC × 1.5 = 15 AC = 15 ÷ 1.5 = 10 AC = 10 cm	Side AC corresponds to RQ (both opposite the 100° angle). So AC × 1.5 = RQ
To find PR: 5 × 1.5 = PR 7.5 = PR PR = 7.5 cm	Side PR corresponds to AB. So AB × 1.5 = PR

Example 2
Triangles ABC and ADE are similar.

Work out the lengths of:

a) BC   b) AC

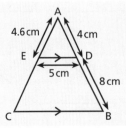

a) A 12 cm C B A 4.6 cm / 4 cm E 5 cm D	It can help to draw the two triangles separately.
AB = 4 + 8 = 12 cm Scale factor = AB ÷ AD = 12 ÷ 4 Scale factor = 3	Side AB corresponds to side AD. You can use these to find the scale factor.
ED × 3 = BC 5 × 3 = 15 cm	Side BC corresponds to side ED.
b) AE × 3 = AC 4.6 × 3 = 13.8 cm	Side AC corresponds to side AE. Notice that you can also work out EC = AC – 4.6 = 9.2 cm

Fluency

1   a)   Explain why triangles MNP and QRS are similar.

    b)   Work out the length of NM.

2   In each part, the triangles are similar.

    Work out the unknown lengths, *a* and *b*.

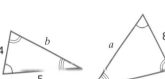

    a)

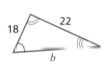

    b)

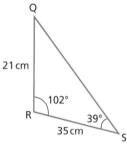

3   In each part, the triangles are similar.

    Work out the unknown lengths, *x* and *y*.

    a)

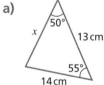
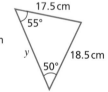

    b)

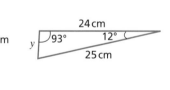

Further

1   Triangles ABC and ADE are similar.

    a)   Calculate the length DE.   (2 marks)

    b)   Calculate the length BD.   (2 marks)

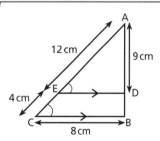

2   Show that triangles A and B are similar.   (2 marks)

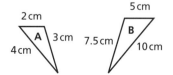

3   Calculate the lengths AX and BC.   (3 marks)

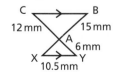

4   Show that triangles PQR and PYZ are similar.   (2 marks)

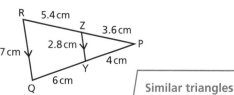

Foundations

1 Work out:

a) 4^2 b) 15^2 c) 6.5^2 d) 1.2^2

2 Work out the following, rounding your answers to 1 decimal place where necessary.

a) $\sqrt{25}$ b) $\sqrt{17}$ c) $\sqrt{42}$ d) $\sqrt{124}$

Facts

Pythagoras' theorem states that 'in a right-angled triangle, the square on the hypotenuse is equal to the sum of the squares on the other two sides'.

In this example, the sides of the triangle have lengths 3 units, 4 units and 5 units.

$3^2 + 4^2 = 5^2$

$9 + 16 = 25$

This can be generalised by labelling the sides of the triangle as a, b and c, where c is always the hypotenuse.

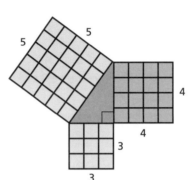

$a^2 + b^2 = c^2$ | This can be written as $a^2 + b^2 = \text{hyp}^2$ if you prefer. See the two examples. |

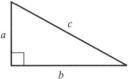

Focus

Example 1
Find the length of the side labelled x.

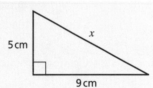

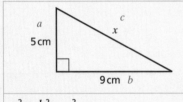	Label the sides a, b and c. Make sure that c is the hypotenuse.
$a^2 + b^2 = c^2$	Or you can use $a^2 + b^2 = \text{hyp}^2$
$5^2 + 9^2 = x^2$	Substitute the values you know into the formula for Pythagoras'
$25 + 81 = x^2$	theorem and solve for x.
$106 = x^2$	
$x = \sqrt{106}$	
$x = 10.3\,\text{cm}$	

Example 2
ABC is an isosceles triangle.

Work out its area.

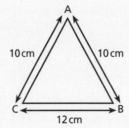

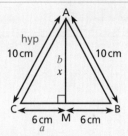

Pythagoras' theorem only applies to right-angled triangles. Start by drawing a line to split the triangle into two right-angled triangles and label the sides of one of them.

$a^2 + b^2 = \text{hyp}^2$	You can use either triangle ABM or ACM as both are right-angled.
$x^2 + 6^2 = 10^2$ $x^2 + 36 = 100$ $x^2 = 100 - 36$ $x^2 = 64$ $x = \sqrt{64}$ $x = 8\,\text{cm}$	Substitute the values you know into the formula for Pythagoras' theorem and solve for x.
Area $= \frac{1}{2} \times 12 \times 8 = 48\,\text{cm}^2$	Use the formula $\frac{1}{2} \times$ base $\times$ height to find the area of the isosceles triangle.

Fluency

1 Calculate the length marked x in each triangle. Give your answers to 1 decimal place.

a)

b)

c)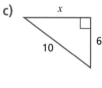

2 Calculate the length of BD, correct to 2 decimal places.

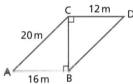

3 ABCD is a rectangle.

a) Calculate the length of AB.

b) Work out the area of the rectangle.

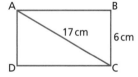

4 ABC is an isosceles triangle.

a) Calculate the perpendicular height, h, of the triangle, correct to 1 decimal place.

b) Calculate the area of the triangle, correct to 1 decimal place.

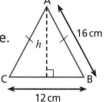

5 ABCD is a square.

The diagonal of the square measures 10 cm.

Calculate the length of one side of the square.

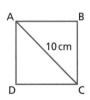

Further

1 ABCDEFGH is a cuboid.

a) Calculate the length FC. Give your answer to 2 decimal places.   (2 marks)

b) Calculate the length EC. Give your answer to 2 decimal places.   (2 marks)

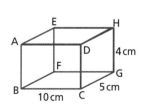

2 A box is a cuboid with dimensions 12 cm, 4 cm and 4 cm.

Will a pencil measuring 15 cm fit into the box?   (4 marks)

Foundations

Name the marked angles using three-letter notation.

a)

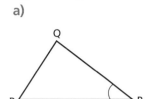

b)

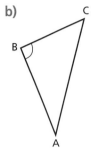

c)

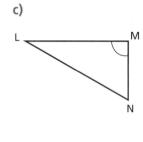

Facts

You can label the sides of a right-angled triangle relative to a given angle x. The **hypotenuse** is opposite the right angle and the other sides are either **opposite** or **adjacent** to the given angle.

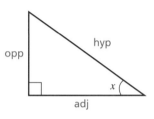

For any given angle, the **ratios** of the lengths of the sides in right-angled triangles are constant.

These ratios are called the **sine**, **cosine** and **tangent** ratios and are defined as follows:

$$\sin x = \frac{\text{opposite}}{\text{hypotenuse}} \qquad \cos x = \frac{\text{adjacent}}{\text{hypotenuse}} \qquad \tan x = \frac{\text{opposite}}{\text{adjacent}}$$

These values are stored in your calculator. You can use these ratios to work out missing sides and angles in right-angled triangles.

Focus

Example 1
Work out the length of the side AB.

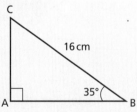

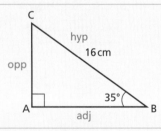

	First, label the sides of the triangle as opposite (opp), adjacent (adj) and hypotenuse (hyp), using the given 35° angle to decide which is which.
$\cos x = \frac{\text{adj}}{\text{hyp}}$	Here you know the hypotenuse and want to find the adjacent, so you need to use the cosine ratio.
$\cos 35° = \frac{AB}{16}$	Substitute in the information you know.
$16 \times \cos 35° = AB$	Rearrange the equation to find AB.
$AB = 13.1$ cm	Use your calculator to find the answer.

Make sure your calculator is set up to work in degrees.

Example 2
Work out the length of the side PR.

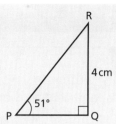

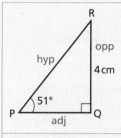	First, label the sides of the triangle as opposite (opp), adjacent (adj) and hypotenuse (hyp), using the given 51° angle to decide which is which.
$\sin x = \frac{\text{opp}}{\text{hyp}}$	Decide which ratio to use and write it down. Here you know the opposite and want to find the hypotenuse, so you need to use the sine ratio.
$\sin 51° = \frac{4}{PR}$	Substitute in the information you know.
$PR \times \sin 51° = 4$ $PR = \frac{4}{\sin 51°}$	Rearrange to solve for PR.
$PR = 5.15 \text{ cm}$	Use your calculator to find the answer and round sensibly.

Fluency

1 Work out the length of the sides marked x. Give your answers correct to 1 decimal place.

a)   b) 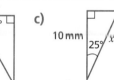 c)   d) 1.3 cm e)   f)

2 Work out the length of BD.

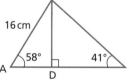

Hint: You need to work out CD first.

3 The diagram shows a ladder standing on horizontal ground.

The length of the ladder is 6 m. The ladder is placed at an angle of 75° to the ground.

How high up the wall will the ladder reach?

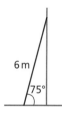

Further

1 ABCD is a quadrilateral.

Calculate the length of CD. (4 marks)

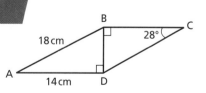

2 a) Calculate the length of BC. (2 marks)

b) Calculate the length of CD. (2 marks)

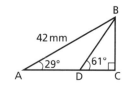

3 Calculate the length of AB, giving your answer to 2 decimal places. (3 marks)

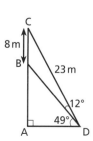

Foundations

Complete the formulae using the words hypotenuse, adjacent and opposite.

$\sin x =$ ——— $\cos x =$ ——— $\tan x =$ ———

Facts

As seen in unit 4.11, for any given angle, the ratios of the lengths of the sides in right-angled triangles are constant.

When you know the ratio and need to work out the angle, you need to use the **inverse** of the ratios, written $\sin^{-1}$, $\cos^{-1}$ and $\tan^{-1}$. This usually means using the 'inverse', 'shift' or '2nd function' key on your calculator. Make sure you know how your calculator works by checking the answers to the examples.

Focus

Example 1

Work out the size of angle x.

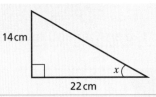

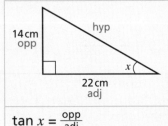	First, label the triangle using the missing angle x to determine the labels.
$\tan x = \frac{opp}{adj}$	Use the labelling to decide which ratio you need to use. Here you know the opposite and adjacent, so you need to use the tangent ratio. Write down the ratio.
$\tan x = \frac{14}{22}$	Substitute in the information you know.
$x = \tan^{-1}\left(\frac{14}{22}\right)$ $x = 32.5°$	If you know a ratio, you use the inverse function on your calculator to find the angle. Here, the inverse of tangent is denoted as $\tan^{-1}$.

Example 2

A ladder of length 4 m rests against a wall. The base of the ladder is 1.5 m from the wall, as shown in the diagram.

Calculate the size of the angle the ladder makes with the ground.

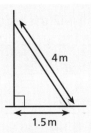

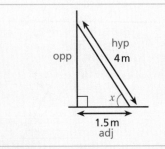	First, identify the angle you have been asked to find and label the sides of the triangle relative to that angle.

$\cos x = \frac{\text{adj}}{\text{hyp}}$	Decide which ratio you need to use and write it out. Here, you know the adjacent and hypotenuse so you need to use the cosine ratio.
$\cos x = \frac{1.5}{4}$	Substitute in the information you know.
$x = \cos^{-1}\left(\frac{1.5}{4}\right)$ $x = 67.9756\ldots$ $x = 68°$ to the nearest degree	Use the inverse function on your calculator to find x.

Fluency

1 Find the sizes of the missing angles marked with a letter in these triangles. Give your answers to 1 decimal place.

a)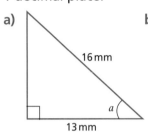

b)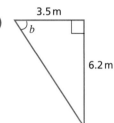

3.5 m
6.2 m
b

c)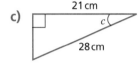

21 cm
28 cm
c

d)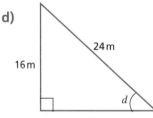

24 m
16 m
d

2 a) Work out the length of BD.

b) Calculate the size of angle BCD.

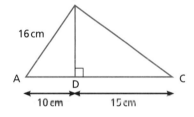

3 a) Work out the length of BD.

b) Work out the size of angle BAD.

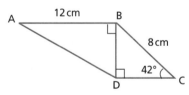

Further

1 Calculate the size of angle x. (3 marks)

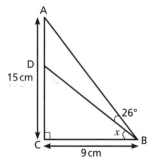

2 ABCD is an isosceles trapezium.

a) Calculate the length of AE. (2 marks)

b) Hence, calculate the size of angle CDA. (2 marks)

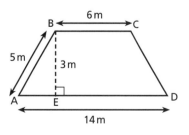

Foundations

Work out the sizes of the angles marked with letters.

a)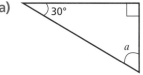

b)

c)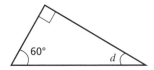

Facts

The trigonometric ratios for some angles can be worked out using special triangles.

In a right-angled isosceles triangle with two sides of 1 cm, using Pythagoras' theorem you can calculate the length of AC to be $\sqrt{2}$ cm.

Now you can label the sides of the triangle relative to one of the 45° angles:

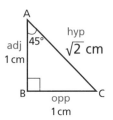

You can use the definitions of sine, cosine and tangent ratios to find:

$$\sin 45° = \frac{\text{opp}}{\text{hyp}} = \frac{1}{\sqrt{2}} \qquad \cos 45° = \frac{\text{adj}}{\text{hyp}} = \frac{1}{\sqrt{2}} \qquad \tan 45° = \frac{\text{opp}}{\text{adj}} = \frac{1}{1} = 1$$

Here are the values you need to know:

	0°	30°	45°	60°	90°
sin x	0	$\frac{1}{2}$	$\frac{1}{\sqrt{2}}$ or $\frac{\sqrt{2}}{2}$	$\frac{\sqrt{3}}{2}$	1
cos x	1	$\frac{\sqrt{3}}{2}$	$\frac{1}{\sqrt{2}}$ or $\frac{\sqrt{2}}{2}$	$\frac{1}{2}$	0
tan x	0	$\frac{1}{\sqrt{3}}$ or $\frac{\sqrt{3}}{3}$	1	$\sqrt{3}$	undefined

You need to know these to be able to solve problems without a calculator.

Focus

Example
Calculate the exact length of AB.

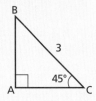

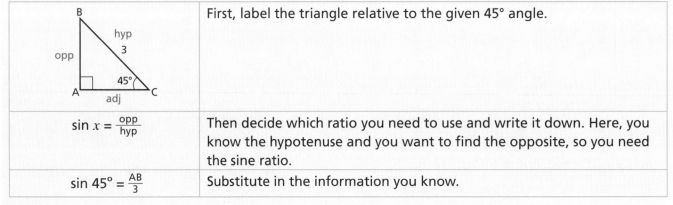

	First, label the triangle relative to the given 45° angle.
$\sin x = \frac{\text{opp}}{\text{hyp}}$	Then decide which ratio you need to use and write it down. Here, you know the hypotenuse and you want to find the opposite, so you need the sine ratio.
$\sin 45° = \frac{AB}{3}$	Substitute in the information you know.

$\frac{1}{\sqrt{2}} = \frac{AB}{3}$	Since you know $\sin 45° = \frac{1}{\sqrt{2}}$, substitute this into the equation.
$\frac{1}{\sqrt{2}} \times 3 = AB$	Rearrange to solve for AB.
$AB = \frac{3}{\sqrt{2}}$	This can also be written as $\frac{3\sqrt{2}}{2}$

If the question asks for an **exact** answer, you will lose marks if you only give a rounded answer.

Fluency

1 An equilateral triangle with side lengths of 2 cm can be used to find exact values for the trigonometric ratios of 30° and 60°

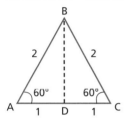

a) State the size of angle ABD.

b) Use Pythagoras' theorem to find the length of BD. Give your answer in exact form.

c) Use triangle ABD to find the following exact trigonometric ratios:

  i) cos 30°   ii) sin 30°   iii) tan 30°

  iv) cos 60°   v) sin 60°   vi) tan 60°

2 Write down the value of sin 30° + tan 45°

3 Calculate the length of AC.

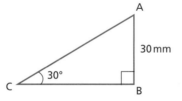

4 Calculate the length of AB.

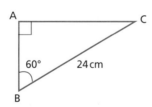

Further

1 Without using a calculator, work out the value of the angle marked x.   (2 marks)

2 Work out the length of AC.   (2 marks)

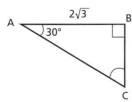

3 Work out the value of cos 30° + sin 60°   (2 marks)

Exact trigonometric values

4.14 Vectors

Foundations

Work out:
          a) 6×-4
          b) $-6 + 4$
          c) $-6 - -4$
          d) -6×-4

Facts

The diagram shows the translation of a square by the vector $\binom{2}{-1}$
This means that the square has been translated two units to the right and one unit down.

Vectors are usually represented using a line segment with an arrow showing the direction of the vector. $\overrightarrow{AB}$ indicates the vector starting at A and ending at B.

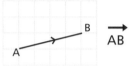

Alternatively, a vector can be denoted using a bold lowercase letter such as **a**.

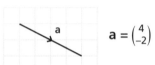

Two vectors are **equal** if they have the same length and are in the same direction.

Two vectors are **parallel** if one vector is a multiple of the other.

Focus

Example 1
Points A and B are marked on the grid.

a) Write the vector $\overrightarrow{AB}$ as a column vector.

b) On a grid, draw the vector $2\overrightarrow{AB}$

c) On a grid, draw the vector $-3\overrightarrow{AB}$

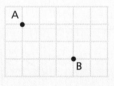

a) 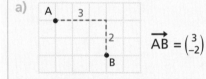 $\overrightarrow{AB} = \binom{3}{-2}$	From A to B is three units to the right and two units down. Now write this using a column vector.
b) $2 \times \overrightarrow{AB} = \binom{6}{-4}$ 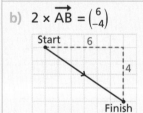	$2\overrightarrow{AB}$ would be $2 \times \binom{3}{-2}$ Now draw this on squared paper. Remember to use the arrow to give the direction of the vector.
c) $-3 \times \overrightarrow{AB} = \binom{-9}{6}$ 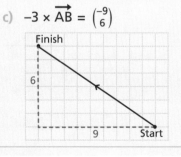	$-3\overrightarrow{AB}$ would be $-3 \times \binom{3}{-2}$ Now draw this on squared paper. Notice that the direction of the vector has now changed.

Example 2

You are given these vectors: $\mathbf{a} = \begin{pmatrix} 2 \\ -6 \end{pmatrix}$ $\mathbf{b} = \begin{pmatrix} 3 \\ 1 \end{pmatrix}$ $\mathbf{c} = \begin{pmatrix} 2 \\ 4 \end{pmatrix}$

Work out:

a) $\mathbf{a} + \mathbf{b}$ b) $2\mathbf{a} - \mathbf{c}$ c) $\mathbf{b} - \mathbf{c}$

d) What does your answer to part c) tell you about the vector $\mathbf{b} - \mathbf{c}$?

a) $\begin{pmatrix} 2 \\ -6 \end{pmatrix} + \begin{pmatrix} 3 \\ 1 \end{pmatrix} = \begin{pmatrix} 5 \\ -5 \end{pmatrix}$	You can add vectors by adding each of the components separately: $2 + 3 = 5$ and $-6 + 1 = -5$
b) $2\mathbf{a} - \mathbf{c} = 2 \times \begin{pmatrix} 2 \\ -6 \end{pmatrix} - \begin{pmatrix} 2 \\ 4 \end{pmatrix} =$ $\begin{pmatrix} 4 \\ -12 \end{pmatrix} - \begin{pmatrix} 2 \\ 4 \end{pmatrix} = \begin{pmatrix} 2 \\ -16 \end{pmatrix}$	First multiply $\mathbf{a}$ by 2, by multiplying both components by 2 Then subtract the components of $\mathbf{c}$.
c) $\begin{pmatrix} 3 \\ 1 \end{pmatrix} - \begin{pmatrix} 2 \\ 4 \end{pmatrix} = \begin{pmatrix} 1 \\ -3 \end{pmatrix}$	On the top row, $3 - 2 = 1$ On the bottom row, $1 - 4 = -3$
d) The vector $\mathbf{b} - \mathbf{c}$ is parallel to the vector $\mathbf{a}$.	The vector $\mathbf{a}$ is $2 \times (\mathbf{b} - \mathbf{c})$ Since $\mathbf{a}$ is a multiple of $\mathbf{b} - \mathbf{c}$, they are parallel vectors.

Fluency

1. The vector $\mathbf{a}$ is given by $\begin{pmatrix} 2 \\ 1 \end{pmatrix}$

   On squared paper draw: a) $\mathbf{a}$ b) $2\mathbf{a}$ c) $-3\mathbf{a}$

2. Write each of these vectors as column vectors.

   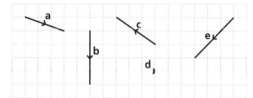

3. The vectors $\mathbf{a}$ and $\mathbf{b}$ are defined as follows:

   $\mathbf{a} = \begin{pmatrix} 6 \\ -2 \end{pmatrix}$ $\mathbf{b} = \begin{pmatrix} 5 \\ 1 \end{pmatrix}$

   Calculate: a) $2\mathbf{a}$ b) $3\mathbf{a} - 2\mathbf{b}$ c) $\mathbf{b} - 2\mathbf{a}$

4. The vectors $\mathbf{p}$ and $\mathbf{q}$ are shown on the grid.

   a) On a grid, draw the vector $-2\mathbf{p}$.

   b) Work out $2\mathbf{p} + 3\mathbf{q}$ as a column vector.

   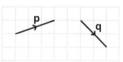

Further

1. A is the point (3, 2) and B is the point (5, 9)

   Write down as a column vector: a) $\overrightarrow{AB}$ (1 mark)   b) $\overrightarrow{BA}$ (1 mark)

2. X is the point (–5, 2) and Y is the point (–6, –2)

   Write down as a column vector: a) $\overrightarrow{XY}$ (1 mark)   b) $-2\overrightarrow{XY}$ (2 marks)   c) $\frac{1}{2}\overrightarrow{YX}$ (2 marks)

3. $\mathbf{p} = \begin{pmatrix} -4 \\ a \end{pmatrix}$ and $\mathbf{q} = \begin{pmatrix} b \\ 2 \end{pmatrix}$

   Given that $2\mathbf{p} - 3\mathbf{q} = \begin{pmatrix} 7 \\ 0 \end{pmatrix}$, work out the values of a and b.   (2 marks)

4. $\mathbf{w} = \begin{pmatrix} 3 \\ -1 \end{pmatrix}$ $\mathbf{x} = \begin{pmatrix} -2 \\ 1 \end{pmatrix}$ $\mathbf{y} = \begin{pmatrix} 22 \\ -8 \end{pmatrix}$

   Show that $3\mathbf{w} - \mathbf{x}$ is parallel to $\mathbf{y}$.   (3 marks)

Facts

The **probability** of something happening tells you how likely it is to happen.

A probability can be expressed as a fraction, a decimal or a percentage. Avoid using ratios and phrases such as '1 out of 3' or '1 in 10' to describe a probability.

Probabilities are always between 0 and 1 (or 0% and 100% if using percentages).

A probability of **0** means the outcome will never happen (it is impossible).

A probability of **1** means the outcome will always happen (it is certain).

When all outcomes are equally likely (such as the outcomes of a fair spinner, dice or coin), then:

$$\text{Probability} = \frac{\text{Number of ways the outcome could happen}}{\text{Total number of possible outcomes}}$$

P(A) is a shorthand way of writing 'the probability that A happens'.

The probabilities of all possible events add up to 1. This leads to two useful results:

P(outcome happens) + P(outcome doesn't happen) = 1
and
P(outcome doesn't happen) = 1 – P(outcome happens)

You can use probabilities to estimate the **expected** number of times an outcome will happen.

Expected frequency of an outcome = probability of the outcome × number of trials

For example, if you roll a fair dice 300 times:

P(rolling a 3) = $\frac{1}{6}$ as all six outcomes are equally likely and there is one 3 on the dice.

The expected number of 3s will be $\frac{1}{6}$ × 300 = 50

This does not mean there will be exactly 50 3s, but this is the best estimate for the number of 3s you will get in 50 rolls of the dice.

Sometimes, to work out probabilities, it is useful to draw a **sample space** diagram that shows all the possible outcomes.

For example, when a fair spinner labelled 1, 2 and 3 is spun twice and the total of the two scores is found, you could draw a sample space like this:

+	1	2	3
1	2	3	4
2	3	4	5
3	4	5	6

You can now see the nine equally likely outcomes and work out, for example,

P(score is greater than 4) = $\frac{3}{9} = \frac{1}{3}$

If a question asks, you should give your answers as simplified fractions, but otherwise you don't have to simplify.

Practice

1. The spinner is spun once.

   What is the probability that it lands on the following?

   a) 1   b) 3   c) 1 or 3   d) an odd number   e) a prime number

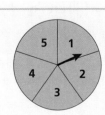

❷ The spinner shown in question 1 is spun twice.

   a) Draw a sample space diagram to show the possible totals of the numbers shown on the spinner.

   b) What is the probability that the total score is:

      i) less than 5?   ii) greater than 7?   iii) even?   iv) greater than 10?

❸ Which of these values could not be a probability?

   0.1835   1.4   −0.2 $\frac{3}{4}$ $\frac{4}{3}$ $\frac{1}{2000}$

❹ A coin is biased so that the probability it lands on heads is 0.56

   a) What is the probability that the coin lands on tails?

   b) The coin is flipped 200 times.

      Estimate the number of times the coin lands on heads.

❺ A draw is being held to win a prize. Seb buys 24 of the 400 tickets.

   What is the probability that Seb does not win the prize? Give your answer as a fraction in its simplest form.

❻ A box contains only blue, black and red pens.

   The probability of picking a blue pen is $\frac{2}{5}$ and the probability of picking a black pen is 15%

   What is the probability of picking a red pen? Give your answer as a decimal.

❼ A fair dice is rolled several times. Here are the first 10 results:

   3   1   6   4   6   5   2   6   5   6 $=\overline{10}$ $\frac{1}{6}$

   What is the probability that the dice lands on 6 on the next roll? Explain your answer.

❽ A bag contains red counters, blue counters, yellow counters and green counters.

   A counter is picked at random from the bag.

   The table shows the probability that the counter is red or yellow.

Colour	Red	Blue	Yellow	Green
Probability	0.3	0.2	0.4	0.1

                                               0.3+0.4=0.7

   The probability of picking a blue counter is twice the probability of picking a green counter.

   a) Complete the table.

   b) There are 15 red counters in the bag.

      How many counters are there altogether in the bag? 50   15:0.3   5×2=10
                                                      5:0.1   5×4=20 } =50
                                                        5×1=5

❾ When playing a game, the probability that Amina hits the target is 0.85   15

   a) How many times would you expect Amina to miss the target if she plays the game 400 times?

   b) What assumption have you made?

❿ There are only boys and girls in a chess club.

   12 of the 40 members are girls and two-thirds of the 15 sixth-formers in the club are boys.

   a) Show this information as a frequency tree. | See unit 5F2 for details about frequency trees. |

   b) Find the probability that a member of the chess club selected at random is a boy who is not in the sixth-form.

Facts

Statistical diagrams are used to represent data visually.

In a **bar chart**, the height of the bar is proportional to the frequency of the item. More than one set of data can be shown on a multiple bar chart.

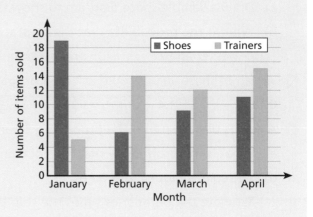

In a **pie chart**, the area of the sector is proportional to the frequency.

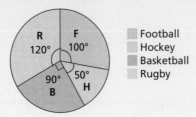

A **scatter diagram** is used to show **bivariate** data. You can see whether there is any **correlation** between the two variables.

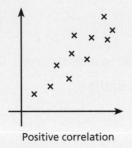
Positive correlation

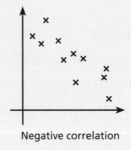
Negative correlation

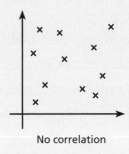
No correlation

You can use a **line of best fit** to estimate one value given another.

A line of best fit is a straight line that is drawn as close to the points as possible. Notice that the line does not need to go through the origin.

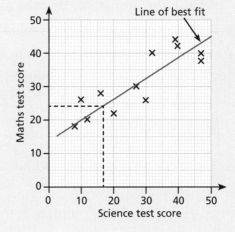

Frequency trees and **Venn diagrams** can be used to organise information.

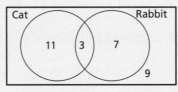

A **time series graph** shows how data changes over time.

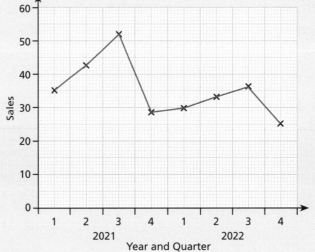

Practice

1. The dual bar chart shows information about how many students belong to the film club and the book club in Years 7, 8 and 9.

   Find the difference between the total number of students in the two clubs.

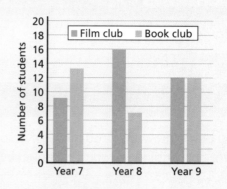

2. Some students were asked if they had a pet.

   The Venn diagram shows the results.

   A student is selected at random.

   Find the probability that the student has:

   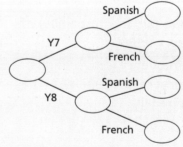

   a) both a cat and a dog   b) a dog   c) no pet   d) a cat but not a dog

3. The table shows information about the eye colours of 120 students.

Eye colour	Blue	Brown	Green	Other
Frequency	46	51	15	8

   Draw a pie chart to represent this information.

   > Hint: the angles in the pie chart will add up to 360°

4. There are 390 students altogether in Years 7 and 8.

   They all study either French or Spanish, but not both.

   Of the 205 students in Year 8, 94 study French.

   In total, 180 students study French.

   Complete the frequency tree.

5. The scatter graph shows the age of a car and its value.

   a) Describe the correlation between the age of a car and its value.

   b) Use the graph to estimate the value of a car that is 5 years old.

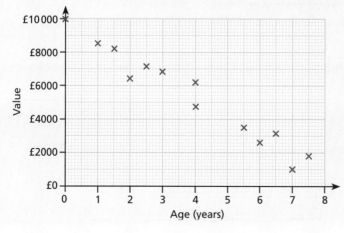

5.1 Relative frequency

Foundations

1 Express 14 as a fraction of 40

2 Work out $\frac{3}{5}$ of 800

Facts

When you don't know the probability of an outcome, you can find an estimate by performing an experiment and finding its **relative frequency**. This is the proportion of the times it occurs in the experiment.

$$\text{Relative frequency} = \frac{\text{number of times the event occurs}}{\text{total number of trials}}$$

The greater the number of trials, the more accurate the estimate of the probability is going to be.

Focus

Example 1

The table shows the results of rolling a six-sided dice 100 times.

Score	1	2	3	4	5	6
Frequency	11	33	14	15	14	13

a) What is the relative frequency of rolling a 2?   b) Do you think the dice is fair?

a) Relative frequency = $\frac{33}{100}$ = 0.33	You can use the formula for relative frequency to estimate probability.
b) If the dice were fair, the probability of a 2 would be $\frac{1}{6}$ = 0.1666… The relative frequency is much higher than the theoretical probability so the dice may not be fair.	One way to decide is to compare the relative frequencies to the theoretical probabilities of a fair dice. Here it is good enough to compare just using the number 2, as it occurs so many more times than the other values.

Example 2

A biased coin is thrown 1000 times.

The graph shows the relative frequency of throwing 'heads' after 200, 400, 600, 800 and 1000 throws.

a) Which is the best estimate of the probability of throwing heads with this coin?

0.8   0.5   0.72   0.7   0.732

b) How many more heads were obtained in the first 400 throws than you would expect for a fair coin?

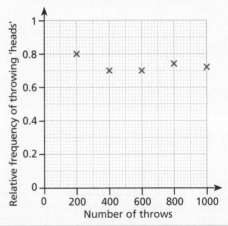

a) 0.72	The best estimate is after the greatest number of trials, 1000
b) 400 × 0.7 = 280	After 400 trials, the relative frequency is 0.7
400 × 0.5 = 200	If the coin were fair, the probability would be 0.5
280 − 200 = 80	Find the difference between these two values.

Fluency

1. Some coloured counters are in a bag. On 200 occasions, a counter is selected at random, its colour noted and the counter is returned to the bag. The results are shown in the table.

Outcome	Red	Yellow	Blue
Frequency	60	125	15
Relative frequency	$\frac{60}{200} = 0.3$		

Complete the table to show the relative frequency for each colour.

2. The spinner is spun 1600 times.

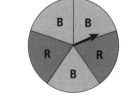

   a) If the spinner is fair, estimate how many times it will land on red.

   The spinner actually lands on red 608 times.

   b) Find the relative frequency of landing on red.

3. A spinner is divided into three equal sections, as shown.

   Rosie spins the spinner 120 times. The spinner lands on red 30 times, green 46 times and blue 44 times.

   a) Explain why the relative frequency of landing on red is 25%

   b) Estimate the probability that the spinner lands on blue.

   c) Is the spinner biased? Give a reason for your answer.

4. A fair spinner is split into five equal sections labelled 1 to 5. The spinner is spun 300 times.

   The relative frequency of landing on the number 4 is 0.39

   How many times did the spinner land on the number 4?

Further

1. Emily is practising netball. She throws six sets of 10 balls from the same point, and notes how many times she scores a goal. Here are her results: 8   6   7   10   6   8

   a) Complete the table.   (2 marks)

Total number of throws	10	20	30	40	50	60
Total number of goals	8	14				
Relative frequency of scoring a goal	0.8					

   b) Draw a graph to show how the relative frequency of scoring a goal changes.   (2 marks)

   c) Estimate the probability that Emily scores a goal.   (1 mark)

2. There are 20 coloured balls in a bag. One ball is chosen at random and then replaced in the bag. The results are shown in the table below.

Colour	Green	Red	Blue	Yellow
Frequency	8	29	44	19

Estimate how many balls of each colour there are in the bag.   (3 marks)

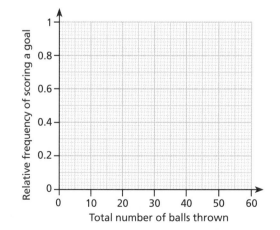

3. A biased coin is thrown x times and it lands on heads y times.

   a) Write an expression for the relative frequency of the coin landing on heads.   (2 marks)

   b) The coin is thrown 100 times.

   Write an expression for the number of times you would expect the coin to land on heads.   (1 mark)

5.2 Combined events

Foundations

Calculate: a) $\frac{1}{3} \times \frac{1}{5}$ b) $\frac{2}{3} \times \frac{4}{5}$ c) $\frac{7}{10} \times \frac{6}{9}$ d) 0.3×0.2

Facts

Independent events do not affect each other. For example, the outcomes of throwing a coin and rolling a dice are independent of each other.

The **sample space** diagram shows the outcomes of rolling a fair six-sided dice and spinning a fair spinner with three different coloured sections.

The probability of rolling a 3 is $\frac{1}{6}$

The probability of spinning blue is $\frac{1}{3}$

From the sample space we can see that the probability of rolling 3 **and** spinning blue is $\frac{1}{18}$

Notice that P(3 and blue) = $\frac{1}{6} \times \frac{1}{3} = \frac{1}{18}$

If events A and B are independent then P(A and B) = P(A) × P(B)

		Spinner		
		Red	Green	Blue
Dice	1	(1, R)	(1, G)	(1, B)
	2	(2, R)	(2, G)	(2, B)
	3	(3, R)	(3, G)	(3, B)
	4	(4, R)	(4, G)	(4, B)
	5	(5, R)	(5, G)	(5, B)
	6	(6, R)	(6, G)	(6, B)

Focus

Example 1

Two fair six-sided dice are rolled.

Find the probability that both show a score greater than 2

P(both > than 2) = P(1st > 2) × P(2nd > 2) $= \frac{4}{6} \times \frac{4}{6} = \frac{16}{36} = \frac{4}{9}$ You don't have to simplify fractions when calculating probabilities unless you are asked to.	The probability of rolling greater than 2 on one dice is $\frac{4}{6}$, as there are four numbers greater than 2 The outcomes of the two dice are independent.

Example 2

a) A and B are independent events.   P(A) = 0.65   P(B) = 0.2

   Work out P(A and B)

b) C and D are independent events.   P(C) = 0.8   P(C and D) = 0.32

   Find P(D)

a) P(A and B) = P(A) × P(B) = 0.65 × 0.2 = 0.13	Use the probabilities given in the question.
b) P(C and D) = P(C) × P(D) 0.32 = 0.8 × P(D) $\frac{0.32}{0.8}$ = P(D) P(D) = 0.4	Use the probabilities given in the question to set up an equation. Rearrange the equation to find P(D).

Fluency

1. Two fair six-sided dice are rolled.

   Calculate the probability that:

   a) both show an even score

   b) neither show a 6

   c) both show a score greater than 4

2. The spinners are both split into equal sectors.

   Work out the probability of:

   a) P(both spinners landing on yellow)

   b) P(both spinners landing on blue)

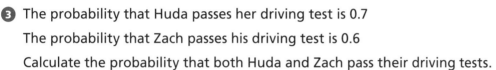

3. The probability that Huda passes her driving test is 0.7

   The probability that Zach passes his driving test is 0.6

   Calculate the probability that both Huda and Zach pass their driving tests.

4. A fair coin is thrown three times.

   a) Find the probability that the coin lands on heads all three times.

   b) Deduce the probability that the coin lands on tails at least once.

5. A computer generates three random digits from 0 to 9 inclusive.

   Work out the probability that:

   a) all three digits are 7s

   b) all three digits are the same

   c) all three digits are odd

Further

1. Tiff says, "You are less likely to roll two 6s on two fair dice than two 5s."

   Is Tiff correct? Explain your answer. (1 mark)

2. A and B are independent events. $P(A) = \frac{5}{6}$ $P(B) = \frac{7}{8}$

   Calculate the probability that:

   a) both A and B occur (2 marks)

   b) neither A nor B occur (2 marks)

3. Bag A contains 7 blue counters and 2 yellow counters.
   Bag B contains 3 blue counters and 4 yellow counters.
   A counter is chosen at random from each bag.

   Bag A   Bag B

   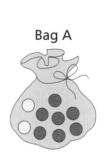

   Calculate the probability that:

   a) both counters are blue (2 marks)

   b) one counter is blue and the other is yellow (2 marks)

4. A box of chocolates contains 7 milk chocolates and 5 dark chocolates.

   A chocolate is taken at random and eaten.

   Another chocolate is then chosen and eaten.

   Find the probability that both the chocolates eaten are dark chocolates. (3 marks)

5.3 Tree diagrams

Foundations

Work out: a) $\frac{3}{13} + \frac{5}{13}$ b) $\frac{3}{13} \times \frac{5}{13}$ c) $1 - \frac{7}{13}$

Facts

Tree diagrams are used to represent probability problems based on two or more events.

This tree diagram represents a bag with 5 red counters and 4 blue counters. A counter is chosen at random then replaced. Another counter is then chosen.

> The probabilities for each set of branches must sum to 1

You can then use the tree diagram to help work out probabilities using the multiplication rule from unit 5.2

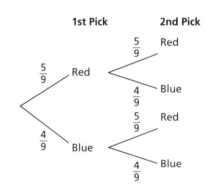

Focus

Example

There are 3 black shirts and 5 white shirts in a drawer.

A shirt is chosen at random, then put back in the drawer.

Another shirt is then chosen.

a) Complete the tree diagram.

b) Work out the probability that:

    i)   both shirts are white

    ii)   one shirt of each colour is chosen

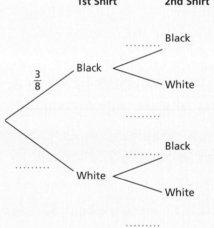

a)	
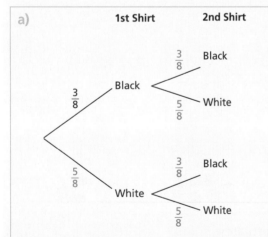	There are 5 white shirts out of a total of 8 shirts. The probability of choosing a white shirt is $\frac{5}{8}$ This is the same for each branch representing a white shirt chosen in the diagram. The probability of choosing a black shirt is $\frac{3}{8}$
b) i) P(both white) = P(white) × P(white) $= \frac{5}{8} \times \frac{5}{8} = \frac{25}{64}$	This corresponds to the bottom branch of the tree diagram. As the colour of the second shirt is independent of the colour of the first shirt, you can use the multiplication rule.

> ii) P(one shirt of each colour)
> = P(1st is black, 2nd is white)
> + P(1st is white, 2nd is black)
> = $\frac{3}{8} \times \frac{5}{8} + \frac{5}{8} \times \frac{3}{8}$
> = $\frac{15}{64} + \frac{15}{64} = \frac{30}{64} = \frac{15}{32}$
>
> This corresponds to the 'middle two' branches of the tree diagram.
>
> You can use the multiplication rule to work out the probability of each event and then add the two probabilities together.

Fluency

1st Pick   2nd Pick

① A box contains 3 red pens and 4 blue pens. A pen is chosen at random, then put back. Another pen is chosen at random.

   a) Complete the tree diagram (right).

   b) Work out the probability of choosing a red pen on both picks.

② The probability that a train is late on any day is 0.7

   a) Complete the tree diagram (below right).

   b) Work out the probability that the train will be late on Monday and Tuesday.

   c) Work out the probability that the train will be on time on at least one of the two days.

③ The probability of Alex passing a test is 0.7

   The probability of Mia passing the same test is 0.4

   a) Draw a tree diagram to represent the information.

   b) Work out the probability that:

      i)   both Alex and Mia pass the test

      ii) neither Alex nor Mia pass the test

      iii) at least one of Alex and Mia passes the test

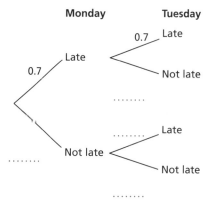

Further

1st Choice   2nd Choice

① A bag contains 3 blue counters, 4 red counters and 6 yellow counters.
   A counter is chosen at random and put back.
   Another counter is then chosen.

   Work out the probability that:

   a) both counters are blue   (2 marks)

   b) both counters are yellow   (2 marks)

   c) at least one blue counter is chosen   (2 marks)

② Kelly needs to take a test to get her new job. The probability she passes is 0.6. If she fails the first time, she is allowed to retake the test. The probability that she passes on her second attempt is 0.75. If she fails the test twice, she will not be offered the job.

   a) Draw a tree diagram to represent this information.   (3 marks)

   b) Work out the probability that Kelly will be offered the job.   (2 marks)

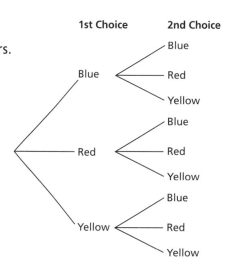

Tree diagrams   105

5.4 Sampling

Foundations

1. Work out $\frac{1}{12}$ of 840

2. Calculate: a) $\frac{13}{21} \times 840$

                b) $\frac{9}{13} \times 840$

Facts

When collecting statistical data, the **population** is the whole group being studied.

As it might be impractical or expensive to study every member of a population, it is more common to select a **sample**. A sample is a smaller group from the population.

A sample is **random** if every member of the population has an equal chance of being selected.

A **biased** sample is one that does not represent the population fairly; for example, leaving out or having too many people from certain groups, such as gender or age. A sample that is too small may also be biased.

The size of each group in a **stratified sample** is proportional to the size of the same group in the population.

Focus

Example 1
Darius is investigating whether people in his town would support the construction of a new sports centre. He selects 10 of his friends to take part in his investigation.

a) What is the population Darius is studying?

b) Give a reason why his sample may be biased.

c) Suggest a way Darius's sample could be improved.

a)	The people who live in his town	The population is the whole group being studied.
b)	His friends might all be his age and the sample might not represent the town as a whole.	You could also say that 10 is a very small sample size.
c)	He could take a random sample of all the people in the town.	You could also suggest a larger sample size.

Example 2
A survey was carried out to see how many investors own cryptocurrency.

22 investors said they did own cryptocurrency and 8 said they did not.

Estimate the number of the 9000 investors in the population that do own cryptocurrency.

$8 + 22 = 30$	Find the total sample size.
$\frac{22}{30}$ said they own cryptocurrency	Find the fraction of the sample who said they own cryptocurrency.
$\frac{22}{30} \times 9000 = 6600$ people	Work out this fraction of the whole population.

Fluency

1 Six people are each given a number from 1–6. A fair six-sided dice is then rolled to choose a person.

Explain why this method selects one of the people at random.

2 Peter wants to know if people who live in his town want a new library. He asks 120 people.

a) What is the population?

b) What is the sample?

3 A school has 2000 pupils. The headteacher wants to know if students enjoy school. He decides to ask 20 students from Year 11.

Give two reasons why this may not be a good sample to use.

4 A company has 230 employees. The owner takes a sample of 92 employees to collect some information.

What percentage of the company's employees does the sample represent?

Further

1 A sample of 45 is taken from a population. The sample represents 30% of the population.

What is the size of the population? (2 marks)

2 A sample of 30 people at a gym are asked which exercise they most prefer. The results are shown in the table.

Exercise	Number of people
Running	17
Cycling	6
Rowing	7

The gym has 800 members in total.

a) Estimate how many of the 800 members prefer each form of exercise. (1 mark)

There was a running club in the gym when this question was asked.

b) How might this affect your answer from part a)? (1 mark)

3 The table shows the number of students in each year group in a school.

Year	7	8	9	10	11
Number of students	140	135	180	142	160

A sample of 50 students is to be selected.

How many Year 9 students should be included in the sample? (2 marks)

4 A scientist wants to track the movements of rats in a city. He captures 50 rats and puts a microchip in them. He then releases these rats.

A week later, he captures 80 rats. 9 of these have a microchip.

Estimate the population of rats in the city. (3 marks)

5.5 Product rule

Foundations

1 Work out 5 × 4 × 3

2 How many possible outcomes are there from throwing a two-sided coin and a six-sided dice?

Facts

If there are *a* ways to do one task and *b* ways to do a second task, then the number of ways to do both tasks is *ab*, the product of *a* and *b*. This is known as the **product rule** and can be applied in lots of different situations; for example, the number of possible outcomes when rolling two ordinary dice is 6 × 6 = 36

In some situations, you need to be careful not to count the same event twice, or you may have to exclude some possibilities.

This sample space shows the outcomes of choosing two students at random from four students.

	Alan	Beatrice	Charlie	Dominique
Alan		(A, B)	(A, C)	(A, D)
Beatrice	(B, A)		(B, C)	(B, D)
Charlie	(C, A)	(C, B)		(C, D)
Dominique	(D, A)	(D, B)	(D, C)	

It is not possible to choose Alan twice.

For each student chosen, there are three other possibilities left for the second student. This gives 4 × 3 = 12 possibilities but, for example, choosing Alan and Beatrice is the same outcome as choosing Beatrice and Alan. Of the 12 outcomes calculated, half of them are repeats so the actual number of possibilities is 12 ÷ 2 = 6

Focus

Example 1
Jack has 7 pairs of shoes and 11 pairs of socks.

How many different combinations of shoes and socks could Jack choose?

7 × 11 = 77	Each of the 7 pairs of shoes can be worn with each of the 11 pairs of socks.

Example 2
Eight hockey teams play matches against each other in a tournament.

Each team plays against each other team once.

How many matches take place?

56 ÷ 2 = 28	For each of the eight teams, there are seven opponents. Calculate 8 × 7 = 56. As all teams play each other once, divide this result by 2 to remove duplicate outcomes.

Fluency

1 Seb has 4 shirts and 3 pairs of trousers.

How many different combinations of shirt and trousers can he choose?

2 There are 17 boys and 13 girls in a class. The teacher wants to choose one boy and one girl at random.

How many different selections can be made?

3 A restaurant has 5 starters, 8 mains and 3 desserts. Kate wishes to choose a starter, main and dessert.

How many different combinations can Kate choose?

4 In a library, there are 56 thriller novels, 27 romance novels and 31 science fiction novels. Abdullah wishes to borrow one of each genre.

How many different combinations of books can he borrow?

5 In a class of 20 students, two students will be chosen randomly to win a prize.

How many different pairs of students can be chosen?

> Remember, choosing student A and student B is the same as choosing student B and student A.

6 How many four-digit numbers are even? | The first digit cannot be zero.

Further

1 Two of the number cards will be chosen at random.

How many different pairs of cards can be chosen?   (2 marks)

2 In a shop, there are 19 bags of crisps and x bottles of drinks to choose from.

The total number of combinations of bags of crisps and drinks is 209

How many drinks are available in the shop?   (2 marks)

3 A sports team is choosing a new kit. There are 4 different shirts, 6 different pairs of shorts and 5 different pairs of socks.

a) How many possible kits are there?   (2 marks)

b) The captain chooses one of the pairs of shorts for the team to wear.

How many possible combinations of kits are there now?   (2 marks)

4 A lock has four digits, each from 0 to 9

a) How many possible combinations of numbers can be used?   (2 marks)

b) How many possible combinations of numbers can be used if no number can be repeated?   (2 marks)

Product rule   **109**

Foundations

Work out: **a)** 50% of 80 **b)** 25% of 120 **c)** 75% of 60 **d)** $\frac{3}{4}$ of 100

Facts

Cumulative frequency shows the total number of items of data so far in a frequency distribution.

Mass, m (kg)	Frequency	Cumulative frequency
$0 < m \leqslant 10$	8	8
$10 < m \leqslant 20$	14	8 + 14 = 22
$20 < m \leqslant 30$	17	22 + 17 = 39
$30 < m \leqslant 40$	3	39 + 3 = 42

There are 22 items with mass up to and including 20 kg. There are 39 items with mass up to and including 30 kg, and 42 items with mass up to and including 40 kg.

A **cumulative frequency diagram** can be drawn to represent the amount of data up to given points in a distribution of data.

You can use a cumulative frequency diagram to estimate:
- the **median**, the middle value of the distribution
- the **lower quartile**, the value below which 25% of the distribution lies
- the **upper quartile**, the value below which 75% of the distribution lies
- any other value you are interested in; for example, a pass mark so that 40% of people pass would correspond to 60% of the data below the pass mark.

The **interquartile range** is found by subtracting the lower quartile from the upper quartile.

Focus

Example
The table shows information about the speeds of 100 vehicles.

a) Draw a cumulative frequency graph to show the information.

b) Estimate the median speed of the vehicles.

c) 20% of the vehicles are exceeding speed x km/h. Estimate the value of x.

Speed, s (km/h)	Cumulative frequency
$0 < s \leqslant 20$	5
$0 < s \leqslant 40$	13
$0 < s \leqslant 60$	39
$0 < s \leqslant 80$	71
$0 < s \leqslant 100$	96
$0 < s \leqslant 120$	100

a)

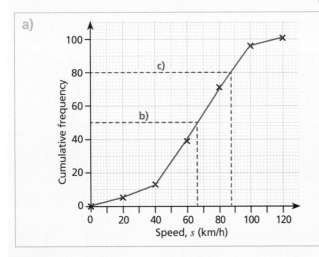

The first point to plot is (0, 0). Then plot the upper bound of each class and the cumulative frequency:

(20, 5), (40, 13), (60, 39), (80, 71), (100, 96) and (120, 100)

Join each point to the previous point with a line segment.

b)	66 km/h	There are 100 vehicles, so the median is at the $\frac{100}{2}$th = 50th position. Use the line labelled b).
c)	88 km/h	As 20% are exceeding speed x, this means 100% – 20% = 80% are going slower than x. Use the line labelled c).

Fluency

1 The table shows information about the wages of 100 people.

a) Draw a cumulative frequency graph.

b) Estimate how many people are paid less than £35

Wage, w (£)	Cumulative frequency
$0 < w \leqslant 20$	4
$0 < w \leqslant 30$	20
$0 < w \leqslant 40$	57
$0 < w \leqslant 50$	85
$0 < w \leqslant 60$	100

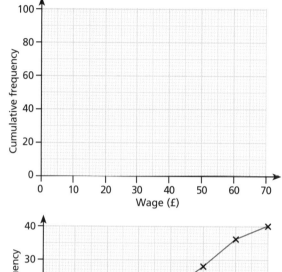

2 The cumulative frequency graph shows the times (in seconds) taken by 40 people to complete a race.

Use the graph to find an estimate for:

a) the median amount of time taken

b) the interquartile range of the times

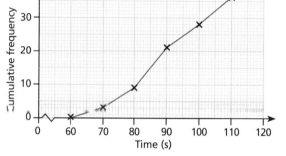

Further

1 The cumulative frequency graph shows the temperatures of 40 containers.

a) Estimate the median temperature. (2 marks)

b) Estimate how many containers had a temperature greater than 50°C (2 marks)

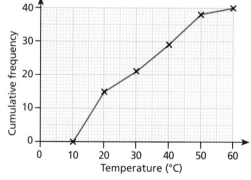

2 The cumulative frequency graph shows information about distances travelled by students each day.

a) How many pieces of data are there? (1 mark)

b) How many students travelled more than 20 miles? (2 marks)

c) Freddie says, "10% of the students travelled 15 miles or more."

Is Freddie correct? Explain your answer. (2 marks)

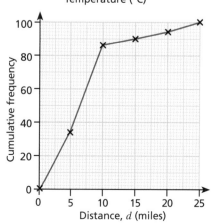

5.7 Box plots

Foundations

Find the median of each set of data.

a) 12   13   17   18   20

b) 54   58   59   89   100

c) 13   14   15   16

Facts

A **box plot** shows key information about a set of data.

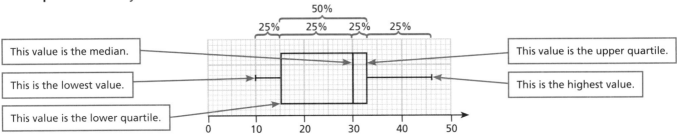

This value is the median.		This value is the upper quartile.
This is the lowest value.		This is the highest value.
This value is the lower quartile.		

The box plot clearly shows the four quarters of a distribution with the box representing the 'middle 50%' of the data.

When comparing box plots from two sets of data, you can see the shapes of the distributions and use the medians to compare average values. You can also use the ranges or interquartile ranges to compare the spread of the data.

Focus

Example

The box plots show the distribution of heights (cm) of students in class A and class B.

Compare the distributions.

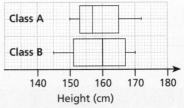

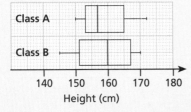

Class A has a median of 157 cm.

Class B has a median of 160 cm.

On average, the heights in class B are higher than the heights in class A.

Comparing medians gives an average height for each class.

Quote the value of the median for each distribution.

The heights of class B are higher on average than class A.

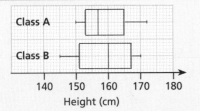

The interquartile range of class A is 12 cm (165–153).

The interquartile range of class B is 16 cm (167–151).

The heights of class A are more consistent.

Comparing the ranges or the interquartile ranges gives the spread of the distribution.

The lower the spread, the more consistent the data is.

Subtract the lower quartile from the upper quartile on each box plot to find the interquartile ranges.

The heights of class A are more consistent as the interquartile range is smaller.

Fluency

1 Use the table to draw a box plot.

Lowest value	5
Lower quartile	19
Median	23
Upper quartile	30
Highest value	34

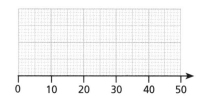

2 The box plots show the masses of some fresh water fish and salt water fish.

Compare the distributions of the masses of the two types of fish.

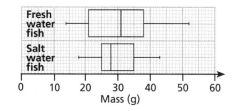

3 The cumulative frequency graph shows the test scores of 40 students in school A.

The box plot shows the test scores of 40 students in school B.

Compare the test scores of school A and school B.

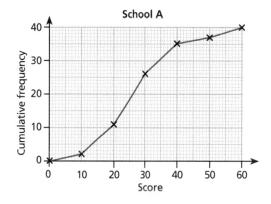

School A

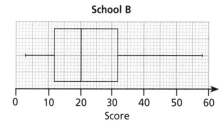

School B

Further

1 The box plot shows the masses of 200 rabbits.

a) Estimate how many rabbits weigh more than 1.3 kg.   (2 marks)

b) Estimate how many rabbits weigh between 0.9 kg and 2.5 kg.   (2 marks)

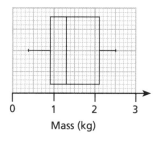

2 Here is some information about the number of hours worked by some people in a week:

- The lowest number is 7 hours.
- The range is 35 hours.
- The median is 20 hours.
- 25% of the employees worked more than 34 hours.
- The interquartile range is 19 hours.

Draw a box plot to show this information.   (3 marks)

5.8 Averages from tables

Foundations

Here are 10 masses: 72 g, 84 g, 70 g, 99 g, 71 g, 80 g, 85 g, 91 g, 78 g, 72 g

Work out: **a)** the mean mass   **b)** the median mass   **c)** the modal mass

Facts

The **mean** is calculated by finding the sum of the data and then dividing by the number of items of data.

The **median** is the middle item in a set of data when the values are written in order.

If there are n items, the median is in the $\left(\frac{n+1}{2}\right)$th position.

The **mode**, or **modal value**, is the most frequent item in a set of data.

Data in tables can be either **discrete** (takes specific values) or **grouped** to cover a range of values (**continuous** data).

Focus

Example 1

The table shows the marks gained by students for a question in an assessment.

Work out:

a) the mean number of marks

b) the median number of marks

c) the modal number of marks

Mark	Frequency
0	5
1	5
2	13
3	24
4	12

a)

Mark	Frequency	Number of marks × frequency
0	5	0
1	5	5
2	13	26
3	24	72
4	12	48
Total	59	151

$\frac{151}{59}$ = 2.6 marks (to 1 d.p.)

Multiply the frequency by the number of marks for each row of the table. This gives the total number of marks for each row.

Work out the total frequency and the total number of marks.

Divide the total number of marks by the total frequency.

b)

Mark	Frequency	Cumulative frequency
0	5	5
1	5	10
2	13	23
3	24	47
4	12	59

The median score is 3

The table contains data for 59 students.

The median is in the $\left(\frac{59+1}{2}\right)$th = 30th position.

The cumulative frequencies show the first 23 items are under 3 and items 24 up to 47 are all 3

> See unit 5.6 for more about cumulative frequency.

c) The modal number of marks is 3

Identify the row with the greatest frequency.

Example 2

The table shows the time taken for students to complete a puzzle.

a) Work out an estimate for the mean time taken.

b) Identify the class containing the median value.

c) Identify the modal class.

Time, t (seconds)	Frequency
$0 < t \leqslant 5$	1
$5 < t \leqslant 10$	7
$10 < t \leqslant 15$	15
$15 < t \leqslant 20$	11
$20 < t \leqslant 25$	5

a)

Time, t (seconds)	Frequency	Midpoint	Midpoint × frequency
$0 < t \leqslant 5$	1	2.5	2.5
$5 < t \leqslant 10$	7	7.5	52.5
$10 < t \leqslant 15$	15	12.5	187.5
$15 < t \leqslant 20$	11	17.5	192.5
$20 < t \leqslant 25$	5	22.5	112.5
Total	39		547.5

Mean $\approx \frac{547.5}{39} = 14.0$ s (to 1 d.p.)

For each row, work out the midpoint of the group.

Multiply the midpoint by the frequency to find an estimate for the total time for each group.

Work out the total frequency and the total time.

Divide the total time by the total frequency.

b) The class containing the median value is $10 < t \leqslant 15$

There are 39 pieces of data so the median will be the $\frac{39+1}{2} = 20$th piece of data. You can add a cumulative frequency column to help.

c) The modal class is $10 < t \leqslant 15$

Identify the row with the greatest frequency.

Fluency

1. The table shows the number of cups of coffee drunk one day by a group of people.

Find: a) the mean

b) the median

c) the mode of the number of cups of coffee drunk

Number of cups	Frequency
0	2
1	7
2	6
3	8
4	4
5	1

2. The table shows some information about how many steps 100 people took one day.

a) Work out the number of people who took between 10 000 and 12 500 steps on that day.

b) Work out an estimate for the mean number of steps taken.

c) Explain why your answer to part b) is an estimate.

Number of steps, x	Number of people
$0 < x \leqslant 2500$	5
$2500 < x \leqslant 5000$	17
$5000 < x \leqslant 7500$	20
$7500 < x \leqslant 10000$	47
$10000 < x \leqslant 12500$	

Further

Subhan measured the heights of 50 trees in a forest. His results are shown in the frequency table.

a) Write down the modal class interval. (1 mark)

b) Work out an estimate for the mean height of the trees measured. (4 marks)

Height, y (metres)	Frequency
$0 < y \leqslant 5$	8
$5 < y \leqslant 15$	25
$15 < y \leqslant 25$	12
$25 < y \leqslant 40$	5

c) Subhan measures 10 more trees that all have heights between 20 m and 25 m.

How would this affect your answers to parts a) and b)? (2 marks)

5.9 Making inferences

Foundations

For each scatter diagram, write whether it shows a positive correlation, a negative correlation or no correlation.

a) 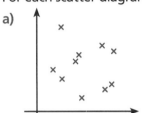   b) 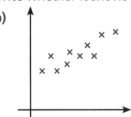   c) 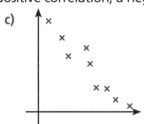   d)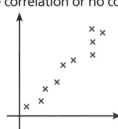

Facts

To make an **inference** means to draw conclusions from a set of data.

Interpolation is to estimate a value within a set of data.

Extrapolation is to estimate a value outside a set of data. Inferences made through extrapolation may not be accurate as you are assuming that the data beyond the existing range will behave in the same way as the given data, which may not be the case.

Where there is a **correlation** between two variables, this does not necessarily mean that one causes the other to happen.

Focus

Example 1

The scatter graph shows the relationship between the outside temperature in degrees Celsius and the number of ice-creams sold in a shop.

a) What type of correlation does the scatter graph show?

b) Estimate the outside temperature when the number of ice-creams sold is 45

Peter estimates that when the outside temperature is 0°C, the number of ice-creams sold is 26

c) Explain why Peter's estimate may not be accurate.

a) Positive correlation	As the value of one variable increases, so does the other.
b) 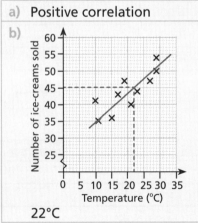 22°C	Draw a line of best fit that follows the trend and has roughly the same number of points on each side. Use a ruler and a pencil to draw a line horizontally from 45 ice-creams until you meet the line of best fit. Then draw a line vertically down to find the corresponding temperature. <div>Your line of best fit may be in a slightly different position. In the exam, a range of answers will be allowed.</div>
c) Peter is using a value outside of the points that have been plotted.	You can't assume that the trend will continue beyond the given data.

Example 2

The scatter graph shows the relationship between the number of bee stings and the number of cups of coffee sold per day in a village.

Aisha says, "The more bee stings per day, the less coffee is sold. This means that people stung by bees buy less coffee."

Explain why Aisha's conclusion may be incorrect.

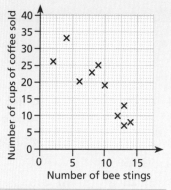

There is a correlation between the variables. This does not mean that one directly affects the other.	Correlation does not imply causation. The correlation in this example is likely to be caused by both variables being affected by the temperature.

Fluency

❶ The table below shows the outside temperature and the number of fans sold on three days. Some information for the fourth day is missing.

Temperature (°C)	10	19	30	
Number of fans sold	6	13	19	40

Sana says, "I think the temperature was approximately 60°C on the day when 40 fans were sold because as the temperature doubles, the number of fans sold doubles as well."

Give a reason why Sana may be incorrect.

❷ The scatter diagram shows the number of people attending a water park and the number of butterflies seen in a garden on 10 days.

a) Describe the correlation shown in the scatter graph.

Euan says, "People are more likely to go to a water park when they see butterflies in their garden."

b) Explain why Euan's conclusion may be incorrect.

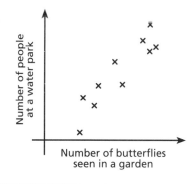

Further

The data in the table shows the handspan and height of 10 adults.

Handspan (cm)	21	18	22	27	16	15	20	17	16	25
Height (m)	1.72	1.70	1.82	1.86	1.64	1.55	1.60	1.64	1.48	1.82

a) Plot a scatter graph for the data in the table.   (2 marks)

b) Describe the relationship between handspan and height.   (1 mark)

c) Use your graph to estimate the height of a person with a handspan of 23 cm.   (2 marks)

d) Explain why your scatter graph may not accurately estimate the handspan of a person 1.98 m tall.   (1 mark)

Answers

Pages 6–7
1F1 Calculations with integers and decimals
Practice

1 **a)** 882   **b)** 1309   **c)** 103.5   **d)** £28.55   **e)** £262.28

2 **a)** 686   **b)** 137   **c)** 25.9   **d)** £8.57   **e)** £112.62

3 **a)** 153 215   **b)** 898 871 < 900 000

4 98.66

5 **a)** 4408   **b)** 436.1   **c)** 54.76

6 £13.76

7 £312.65

8 **a)** 28.3   **b)** 56

9 **a)** 17   **b)** 14

10 £875

11 **a)** −2   **b)** −8   **c)** −8   **d)** −2

12 **a)** 15   **b)** −15   **c)** −5   **d)** −6   **e)** 25

Pages 8–9
1F2 Working with fractions
Practice

1 **a)** $\frac{3}{5}$ **b)** $\frac{31}{75}$ **c)** $\frac{11}{20}$

2 **a)** 0.22   **b)** 0.545   **c)** 0.324

   d) 0.85   **e)** 0.425   **f)** 0.625

3 **a)** $\frac{13}{20}$ **b)** $\frac{78}{125}$ **c)** $\frac{11}{40}$ **d)** $\frac{89}{250}$

4 $\frac{18}{5} = 3\frac{3}{5}$, $3\frac{3}{4} > 3\frac{3}{5}$ as $\frac{3}{4} > \frac{3}{5}$

5 **a)** $\frac{11}{12}$ **b)** $\frac{1}{8}$ **c)** $\frac{7}{12}$ **d)** $\frac{9}{2} = 4\frac{1}{2}$

6 **a)** $3\frac{5}{12}$ **b)** $11\frac{11}{24}$ **c)** $14\frac{2}{3}$

   d) $3\frac{1}{3}$ **e)** $13\frac{1}{3}$ **f)** $2\frac{2}{3}$

7 $\frac{253}{96} = 2\frac{61}{96}\,\text{m}^2$

8 $\frac{84}{95}\,\text{cm}$

9 **a)** 36   **b)** 220

10 $\frac{3}{5}$ of 480 = 288

Pages 10–11
1F3 Working with percentages
Practice

1

Percentage	Fraction	Decimal
40%	$\frac{2}{5}$	0.4
60%	$\frac{3}{5}$	0.6
6%	$\frac{3}{50}$	0.06
5%	$\frac{1}{20}$	0.05
35%	$\frac{7}{20}$	0.35

2 **a)** 20 kg   **b)** 60 g   **c)** 54 m

   d) £2250   **e)** 84 cm   **f)** £2100

3 Example answers:

   50% − 5%

   20% + 25%

   4 × 10% + 5%

9 × 5%

4 **a)** 65.7 kg   **b)** £232.50   **c)** 102 ml

   d) £2520   **e)** £384   **f)** 0.36 kg

   g) £1029.60   **h)** 16.8536 km

5 60% of £300 is £5 greater

6 $66\frac{2}{3}$%

7 47.5%

8 Example answer: $\frac{80}{100} \times 60 = \frac{60}{100} \times 80$

9 0.299   30.5% $\frac{1}{3}$ 35% $\frac{2}{5}$

10 0.4 = 40% > 23%

11 35% of 102 is 35.7 > 36% of 97, which is 34.92

12 £32.50

13 £63

14 35%

15 £3045

Pages 12–13
1.1 Reverse percentages
Foundations

1 **a)** £51.20   **b)** £84.00

2. **a)** $x = 50$ **b)** $x = 60.5$

Fluency

1 **a)** 9   **b)** 4.5   **c)** 36   **d)** 90

2 35

3 £7

4 800

5 80

6 £275

7 £37 423.94

8 £218.25

Further

1 There is a not an integer which can be increased by 40% to give 1640. Therefore, the teacher is incorrect as you cannot have a decimal number representing the number of students.

2 0.65 × 270 = 175

   A = 175.5 ÷ 0.15 = 1170

3 100 ÷ 1.25 = 80

   $\sqrt{80}$ = 8.9 cm

4 **a)** The 15% reduction is applied to 80% of the original, not 100% of the original price.

   b) £64.99

Pages 14–15
1.2 Exact answers
Foundations

1 Radius = 9 mm   Diameter = 18 mm

   Radius = 1.7 m   Diameter = 3.4 m

2 $p = \frac{5}{3}$

Fluency

1 a) $g = \frac{3}{2}$ **b)** $h = \frac{8}{5}$ **c)** $c = \frac{17}{9}$ **d)** $b = \frac{5}{4}$

2 a) Circumference = 100π mm

b) Area = 2500π mm^2

3 EG = $\sqrt{53}$ cm

4 a) $x = \sqrt{11}$ **b)** $w = \sqrt{10}$

5 a) Volume = 6250π m^3

b) Volume = 100π cm^3

6 $\sqrt{18}$ cm

7 a) $\cos 45° = \frac{1}{\sqrt{2}} = \frac{\sqrt{2}}{2}$ **b)** $\tan 45° = 1$

Further

1 $\frac{1}{2} \times \pi \times 30 = 15\pi$

Arc length = 15π

Perimeter $(15\pi + 30)$ cm

2 a) $\sin 45° = \frac{1}{\sqrt{2}}$ **b)** $\cos 30° = \frac{\sqrt{3}}{2}$

c) $\sin 60° = \frac{\sqrt{3}}{2}$ **d)** $\tan 60° = \sqrt{3}$

3 $850 = \frac{1}{3} \times \pi \times 9^2 \times h$

$850 = 27\pi h$

$h = \frac{850}{27\pi}$

4 $\cos 45 = \frac{x}{10}$

$x = 10\cos 45$

$x = 5\sqrt{2}$

$\tan 30 = \frac{y}{6\sqrt{3}}$

$y = 6\sqrt{3} \tan 30$

$y = 6$

Pages 16–17
1.3 Limits of accuracy

Foundations

1 a) 728.6 **b)** 729 **c)** 730 **d)** 700

Fluency

1 a) 6.64, 6.57, 7.05 and 6.599

b) 6.64, 6.57 and 6.599

c) 7.7, 7.54 and 7.706

2 $6.5 \leqslant y < 7.5$

3 $250 \leqslant x < 350$

4 a) Various answers are possible, e.g. 72.5 and 73.1 miles

b) 73 miles

5 a) 39 500

b) 40 499

c) $39\,500 \leqslant n < 40\,500$

6 a) 75 650, 75 900 and 75 050

b) $15 \leqslant x < 16$

7 a) $50 \leqslant n < 150$

b) $95 \leqslant n < 105$

c) $99.5 \leqslant n < 100.5$

Further

1 If the number represents the number of people, the greatest possible value is 649, as it can only be an integer.

If the number represents the length of a table, the greatest possible value can be given to any number of decimal places, e.g. 649.999

The smallest possible value for both is 550

2 Various answers are possible. Examples:

a) A number, g, has been rounded to 70.1 to 1 decimal place. What is the error interval?

b) A number, h, has been rounded to 7910 to the nearest ten. What is the error interval?

c) A number, k, has been rounded to 80 000 to the nearest ten. What is the error interval?

3 a) $7.5\text{cm} \leqslant l < 8.5\text{cm}$

b) $37.5\text{cm} \leqslant p < 42.5\text{cm}$

4 a) $11.6 \leqslant x + y < 11.8$

b) $4.4 \leqslant y - x < 4.6$

Pages 18–19
1.4 Calculator and non-calculator methods

Foundations

1 a) 2 **b)** –8 **c)** –8 **d)** –2 **e)** –2

2 a) 360 000 **b)** 0.00704

Fluency

1 a) 15 **b)** –15 **c)** –5 **d)** –6

2 a) 4 **b)** 3 **c)** $-\frac{3}{2}$

3 a) $1\,900\,000 = 1.9 \times 10^6$

b) $0.00247 = 2.47 \times 10^{-3}$

c) 1.05×10^1

d) $32\,000 = 3.2 \times 10^4$

4 a) $35 \times 10^5 = 3.5 \times 10^6$

b) $49 \times 10^6 = 4.9 \times 10^7$

c) 1.25×10^{-3}

d) $400\,000 - 500 = 399\,500 = 3.995 \times 10^5$

5 a) 5 and –4, 10 and –2

b) Any two of: 10 and –2, –20 and 4, 5 and –1

c) Any two of: –5 and 4, –1 and 2, –2 and 2, –4 and 10, –2 and 10, –1 and 10, 2 and 10, 5 and 10, 4 and 10

Further

1 $-5^2 = -25$ as you square first using the order of operations. $(-5)^2 = -5 \times -5 = 25$, so they are different.

2 $A = 3$ and $B = -8$

3 $(1.5 \times 10^8) \div (3 \times 10^5) = 500 = 5 \times 10^2$ seconds

Pages 20–21
2F1 Understanding algebra

Practice

1 a) $7p$ **b)** $6q$ **c)** $\frac{c}{9}$ **d)** $5t^2$

e) $42k$ **f)** $15mn$ **g)** $30p^2$ **h)** $\frac{10}{m}$

2 a) $8p + 10q$ **b)** $-2p - 2q$ **c)** $-2p + 2q$

3 a) 22　　**b)** 72　　**c)** 144　　**d)** 1.5
　e) 13.5　**f)** −2

4 a) $6x + 3y$　　**b)** $2x^2 + xy$
　c) $6x^2 - 3xy$　**d)** $30xy - 15x^2$

5 a) $33m + 12n$　**b)** $11m - 7n$

6 a) i) $4(2p - 3q)$　**ii)** $y(x + 3z - 9)$
　b) i) $6b(2a - 3c)$　**ii)** $5x(2x - 1)$

7 Both expand to $16p + 32$

8 a) Values of y are −7, −4, −1, 2, 5
　b)

9 a) 33　　　**b)** 2　　　**c)** 9

10 $a = 7$, $b = 2$

Pages 22–23
2F2 Basic equations and inequalities
Practice

1 a) $x = 6.25$　**b)** $x = 8.75$　**c)** $x = 2.5$　**d)** $x = 12.5$
　e) $x = 100$　**f)** $x = 146$　**g)** $x = 154$　**h)** $x = 140$

2 a) $x > 6.25$　**b)** $x < 8.75$　**c)** $x \geqslant 2.5$　**d)** $x < 12.5$
　e) $x \geqslant 100$　**f)** $x < 146$　**g)** $x \geqslant 154$　**h)** $x < 140$

3 66

4 15

5 a) $a = 2$　　**b)** $a = -2$

6 a) $y > 64$　　**b)** $y > 16$　　**c)** $y < -16$

7 $p = 12.5$

8 $t = 9$

9 $x = 27$

10 4

11 4

12 35°

13 8

Pages 24–25
2.1 Changing the subject
Foundations

　a) $x = \frac{18}{5}$ (or equivalent)　　**b)** $x = 90$
　c) $x = \frac{5}{18}$ (or equivalent)　**d)** $x = -13$　**e)** $x = 13$
　f) $x = 3$　　**g)** $x = -3$　　**h)** $x = -49$　**i)** $x = 39$

Fluency

1 a) $x = r - t$　**b)** $x = z - v$　**c)** $x = kw$　**d)** $x = \frac{m}{a}$
　e) $x = \frac{p + 5}{3}$　**f)** $x = \frac{2p}{3g}$　**g)** $x = \frac{12 - w}{7}$　**h)** $x = ag - 3f$
　i) $x = \frac{3b - 4y}{a}$　**j)** $x = \sqrt{\frac{d - 7n}{4}}$
　k) $x = \frac{t^2 - 1}{3}$　**l)** $x = \frac{(y + h)^2}{5}$　**m)** $x = 3z^2 + 7$

2 a) $a = 5(t - 3)$ or $a = 5t - 15$
　b) $t = 5.4$　　**c)** $a = 35$

3 a) $C = 3 + 0.94m$　　**b)** $m = \frac{C - 3}{0.94}$　**c)** 8 miles

Further

1 $h = \frac{2A}{b}$

2 a) $P = 2(3r + \frac{1}{2}q) + 2(4q - r)$
　　　$= 6r + q + 8q - 2r$
　　　$= 4r + 9q$
　b) $q = \frac{P - 4r}{9}$

3 $r = \sqrt{\frac{A}{\pi}}$

4 $C = \frac{5}{9}(F - 32)$

5 a) $h = \frac{3V}{\pi r^2}$
　b) $r = \sqrt{\frac{3V}{\pi h}}$
　c) $r = \sqrt{\frac{3 \times 420}{30\pi}}$
　　　$= 3.65636...$
　　$d = 2r$
　　　$= 7.31\,\text{cm}$ (to 3 s.f.)

Pages 26–27
2.2 Unknowns on both sides
Foundations

1 a) $x = 9$　　**b)** $x = -2$　　**c)** $x = 3$

Fluency

1 a) $a = 7$　　**b)** $b = -1$　　**c)** $c = 2$
2 a) $d = 1$　　**b)** $f = 2$　　**c)** $h = -3$
3 a) $j = 1$　　**b)** $k = 1$　　**c)** $m = 4$
4 a) $p > -2.5$　**b)** $3.5 < p$ or $p > 3.5$　**c)** $2 \geqslant p$ or $p \leqslant 2$
5 a) $a < 1$　　**b)** C

Further

1 $14 = 11 + 2n$
　$n = \frac{3}{2}$

2 $12p - 3 = 4p + 13$
　$8p = 16$
　$p = 2$

3 $8z + 4 = 10z - 8$
　$12 = 2z$
　$z = 6$
　Side length of the square is 13 cm

4 $4x + 5 = 5x - 1$
　$5 = x - 1$
　$x = 6$

5 $10 - 3x > 17 - x$
　$10 > 17 + 2x$
　$-7 > 2x$
　$-3.5 > x$, $x < -3.5$
　So $x = -4$ is the greatest integer

Pages 28–29
2.3 Laws of indices
Foundations

1 a) a^2　　**b)** b^5　　**c)** $6c^3$
2 a) 1000　　**b)** 49　　**c)** 81

Fluency

1 a) $4a^5$ **b)** $35b^3$ **c)** $10c^4 - 4c^3$

2 a) d^{13} **b)** $2f^5$ **c)** g^{30}

   d) $12h^7$ **e)** $54y^3z^9$ **f)** $-8x^2n^5$

   g) $24t^8$ **h)** f

3 a) j^9 **b)** $5k^4$ **c)** $m^{16}n$

   d) $5p^{24}q^8$ **e)** $\dfrac{3r^{-8}}{5}$ **f)** $2d^6$

   g) $\dfrac{5x^{-9}}{6}$ or $\dfrac{5}{6x^9}$ **h)** $\dfrac{5a^{51}b^{-6}}{4}$ or $\dfrac{5a^{51}}{4b^6}$

4 a) p^{12} **b)** h^{30} **c)** $16f^8$

5 a) 36 **b)** 1 **c)** $\dfrac{1}{8}$ **d)** 1

Further

1 a^{-11}

2 $\dfrac{1}{5}m^{14}n^{-7}$ or $\dfrac{m^{14}}{5n^7}$

3 $c = 4$

4 $w = -3$

5 $g^{\frac{43}{60}}$

6 Example answer:

For Amina: $2^5 \times 2^5 = 2 \times 2 \times 2 \times 2 \times 2 \times 2 \times 2 \times 2 \times 2 \times 2 = 2^{10}$

For Rob: $2^5 \times 2^5 = (2 \times 2) \times (2 \times 2) \times (2 \times 2) \times (2 \times 2) \times (2 \times 2)$

$= 4 \times 4 \times 4 \times 4 \times 4 = 4^5$

7 $x = 4$

Pages 30–31
2.4 Expanding and factorising

Foundations

1 a) $2a + 8$ **b)** $b^2 - 3b$ **c)** $2c^2 + 6cd$

2 a) $3(f + 4)$ **b)** $g(g - 5)$ **c)** $5t(t - 3u)$

Fluency

1 a) $a^2 + 11a + 24$ **b)** $b^2 + 5b - 24$ **c)** $c^2 - 5c - 24$

   d) $d^2 - 11d + 24$ **e)** $f^2 - 5f - 24$ **f)** $-g^2 - 5g + 24$

2 a) $(h + 1)(h + 5)$ **b)** $(j + 4)(j + 5)$ **c)** $(k - 5)(k - 2)$

   d) $(l + 12)(l - 2)$ **e)** $(m - 6)(m + 3)$ **f)** $(n + 17)(n - 2)$

   g) $(x + 6)(x - 6)$ **h)** $(y + 10)(y - 10)$ **i)** $(5 + t)(5 - t)$

3 a) $2p^2 + 7p + 3$ **b)** $3q^2 - 5q - 2$ **c)** $4r^2 - 15r - 4$

   d) $12s^2 - 25s + 12$ **e)** $t^2 + 16t + 64$ **f)** $9u^2 - 24u + 16$

Further

1 $2x^2 - 6x + 7x - 21 \equiv 2x^2 + x - 21$

2 $ac + ad + bc + bd$

3 $(x + y)^2 \equiv (x + y)(x + y) \equiv x^2 + 2xy + y^2$

4 $x + 14$

5 $(x + 5)(x + 4)(x + 3) \equiv (x^2 + 9x + 20)(x + 3)$

$\equiv x^3 + 3x^2 + 9x^2 + 27x + 20x + 60$

$\equiv x^3 + 12x^2 + 47x + 60$

6 $(7a + 9b)(7a - 9b)$

Pages 32–33
2.5 Algebraic arguments

Foundations

   a) $x - 5$ **b)** $a + b + c$ **c)** abc **d)** $t - r$

Fluency

1 a) $5n$ **b)** $-3n$ **c)** $2n$

   d) $4n + 1$ **e)** $9n - 2$

2 a) $q + 2$ **b)** $r - 3$

3 a) $6n \equiv 3(2n)$

   b) $20k \equiv 4(5k)$

   c) $15d - 10 \equiv 5(3d - 2)$

4 a) $2p + 3q$

   b) $p + 2p + 3q \equiv 3p + 3q \equiv 3(p + q)$ so 3 × the third term

Further

1 $(3n)^2 = 9n^2 = 9 \times n^2$, so a multiple of 9

2 Example answer: $k + (k + 1) \equiv 2k + 1$, so odd

3 Example answer: $2k(2k + 1) \equiv 4k^2 + 2k \equiv 2(2k^2 + k)$, so multiple of 2 so even

4 Example answer: $(2k + 1)^2 \equiv 4k^2 + 4k + 1 \equiv 4(k^2 + k) + 1$, which is 1 more than a multiple of 4

5 $(n + 5)^2 - (n - 2)^2 \equiv n^2 + 10n + 25 - (n^2 - 4n + 4) \equiv 14n + 21 \equiv 7(2n + 3)$, so multiple of 7

Pages 34–35
2.6 Parallel lines

Foundations

Parallel: AB and CD

Perpendicular: AB and AD, AD and DC

Fluency

1 Example answers:

   a) $x = 4$ **b)** $y = -5$ **c)** $y = 4x + 3$

   d) $y = x - 9$ **e)** $y = -3x + 1$ **f)** $y = 2x + 11$

   g) $y = 10x - 6$ **h)** $y = -6x + 15$

2 $y = 3x + 1$ $y = 3x - 1$

   $y = 2x - 3$ $y = 2x + 8$

   $y = 8 - 2x$ $y = -3 - 2x$

   $y = 2 + 8x$ $y = 8x - 1$

3 Example answers:

   a) $y = 4x - 8$ **b)** $y = -4x + 18$ **c)** $y = -x + 3$

   d) $y = 3x + 2$ **e)** $y = 3x + 5$ **f)** $y = x - 4$

4 A and D

Further

1 a) 0 **b)** 4 **c)** Example answer: $y = 3x + 8$

2 $y = 4x + 10$, $2y = 8x + 16$ and $3y = 12x$

   $4y = x - 10$, $y = \frac{1}{4}x + 10$ and $8y = 2x - 24$

   $y = 10 - 4x$, $y + 4x = 100$ and $5y = -20x$

3 The two lines are exactly the same, i.e. $y = 2x + 13$

4 $y = 5x - 3$

5 a) -1 **b)** $(0, 7)$

Pages 36–37
2.7 Equation of a line

Foundations

1 a) 3 **b)** -5 **c)** 2

2 a) 1   **b)** 3   **c)** –2   **d)** –1.5

Fluency

1 a) $y = 3x - 1$ **b)** $y = x - 5$

   c) $y = -2x - 1$ **d)** $y = -10x + 220$

2 a) $y = 5x - 7$ **b)** $y = 8x + 19$ **c)** $y = -3x - 3$

Further

1 $y = \frac{1}{4}x + 8$

2 $-3x + 4y - 18 = 0$ **or** $3x - 4y + 18 = 0$

3 $y = 5x - 3$

4 $l = 5x - 6$, $q = 4$

Pages 38–39
2.8 Plotting more complex functions

Foundations

Example answer:

x	–2	–1	0	1	2
$y = 3x - 4$	–10	–7	–4	–1	2

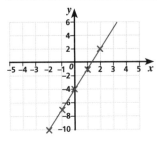

Fluency

1 a)

x	–2	–1	0	1	2
$y = x^3 - 2x$	–4	1	0	–1	4

   b)

2 a)

x	–4	–3	–2	–1	0	1	2	3	4
$y = \frac{2}{x}$	$-\frac{1}{2}$	$-\frac{2}{3}$	–1	–2	undefined	2	1	$\frac{2}{3}$	$\frac{1}{2}$

   b)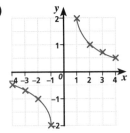

3

x	–3	–2	–1	0	1	2	3
$y = 2^x$	0.125	0.25	0.5	1	2	4	8

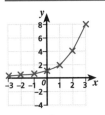

4

Equation	Graph
$y = 3x + 5$	B
$y = \frac{3}{x}$	D
$y = 5 - 3x$	C
$y = x^2 - 4$	A

Further

1 $a = 3$

2 a)

x	–3	–2	–1	0	1	2	3
$y = \frac{1}{x^2}$	$\frac{1}{9}$	$\frac{1}{4}$	1	undefined	1	$\frac{1}{4}$	$\frac{1}{9}$

   b)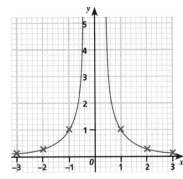

   c) About 1.4

3 $2a^4 = 162$, $a^4 = 81$, $a = 3$

Time (hours)	0	0.5	1	1.5	2	4	10
Number of bacteria (thousands)	2	3.46	6	10.39	18	162	118 098

Pages 40–41
2.9 Roots and turning points

Foundations

   a) $(x + 2)(x + 5)$

   b) $(x + 5)(x - 2)$

   c) $(x - 5)(x + 2)$

Fluency

   a) i) $x = -3$, $x = 1$ **ii)** $(0, -3)$ **iii)** $(-1, -4)$

   b) i) $x = -1$, $x = 3$ **ii)** $(0, -3)$ **iii)** $(1, -4)$

   c) i) $x = 0$, $x = 4$ **ii)** $(0, 0)$ **iii)** $(2, -4)$

   d) i) $x = 2$, $x = -4$ **ii)** $(0, -8)$ **iii)** $(-1, -9)$

   e) i) $x = -2$, $x = 4$ **ii)** $(0, -8)$ **iii)** $(1, -9)$

   f) i) $x = -1$, $x = 3$ **ii)** $(0, 3)$ **iii)** $(1, 4)$

Further

1 a) 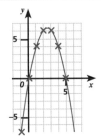   **b)** $(2.5, 6.25)$

c) $x = 0$, $x = 5$

d) $x = 0.7$, $x = 4.3$

2 a) $x = -3.3$, $x = 0.3$

b) $x = -3.8$, $x = 0.8$

Pages 42–43
2.10 Simultaneous equations

Foundations

a) $x = 10.5$ **b)** $y = -\frac{19}{4}$

Fluency

1 a) $x = 3.2$, $y = 2.2$ **b)** $x = 3$, $y = 2$ **c)** $x = -15$, $y = -14$

2 a) $a = 5$, $b = 2.5$ **b)** $a = 5$, $b = 2.5$ **c)** $a = 10.75$, $b = 1.5$

3 a) $h = 0.4$, $j = 1$ **b)** $h = 6.4$, $j = -3$ **c)** $h = -3$, $j = -4$

Further

1 No. When you substitute into the second equation, the solution does not work.

$p = 5$ $r = 3$

$2p - r = 4$

$10 - 3 \neq 4$

2 a) $5h + c = 155$ $8h + c = 230$

$h = £25$ $c = £30$

b) £250 + £30   Total cost = £280

3 $p = £0.48$ $r = £0.90$

Total cost = £9.24

Pages 44–45
2.11 Solving quadratic equations by factorisation

Foundations

1 a) $x - 4$ **b)** $x - 4$ **c)** $x - 2$

2 a) $(x + 2)(x + 1)$ **b)** $(x - 4)(x + 1)$ **c)** $(x - 4)(x - 1)$

Fluency

1 a) $x = 5$ or $x = -1$ **b)** $x = -4$ or $x = 6$ **c)** $x = 5$ or $x = 0$

2 a) $g = -3$ or $g = -1$ **b)** $g = -2$ **c)** $g = 3$ or $g = 1$

3 a) $m = -2$ or $m = 5$ **b)** $m = 2$ or $m = -5$ **c)** $m = \pm 5$

4 a) $x = -13$ or $x = 9$ **b)** $x = -2$ or $x = 9$ **c)** $x = 1$ or $x = 9$

Further

1 $x(x - 3) = 40$

$x^2 - 3x - 40 = 0$

$(x - 8)(x + 5) = 0$

$x = 8$ or $x = -5$ (discount -5 as a negative side length is not possible)

Length = 8 cm

Width = 8 − 3 = 5 cm

2 a) Jakub has not made the equation equal to zero before attempting to solve.

b) $x^2 + 3x - 10 = 0$

$(x + 5)(x - 2) = 0$

$x = -5$ or $x = 2$

3 $(x + 5)(x + 5) = 0$

$x + 5 = 0$

$x = -5$ for each bracket so only one solution

4 Area of a triangle = $\frac{1}{2}$ base × height

$\therefore \frac{1}{2} \times 2x(x + 5) = 14$

$x^2 + 5x - 14 = 0$

$(x + 7)(x - 2) = 0$

$x = -7$ or $x = 2$ (discount the negative solution because x is a length)

$x = 2$ mm

5 a) Area of a trapezium = $\frac{1}{2}(a + b)h$

$\therefore \frac{1}{2}(2x + 14)(x - 2) = 36$

$(x + 7)(x - 2) = 36$

$x^2 + 5x - 14 = 36$

$x^2 + 5x - 50 = 0$

b) $(x + 10)(x - 5) = 0$

$x = -10$ or $x = 5$ (discount the negative solution because x is a length)

$x = 5$

Missing length of the parallel side: 2(5) = 10 m

Difference between the lengths of the parallel sides:

14 − 10 = 4 m

Pages 46–47
2.12 Inequalities and number lines

Foundations

a) $x \leqslant 3$ **b)** $x > 9.5$ **c)** $x < 9$ **d)** $x \geqslant \frac{19}{5}$

Fluency

1 a)

b)

c)

2 a)

b)

c)

3 a) $x \leqslant -2$ **b)** $-2 < x \leqslant 3$ **c)** $-3 < x < 4$

4 a) $-5, -4, -3, -2$ **b)** $-1, 0, 1, 2, 3$ **c)** $-2, -1, 0, 1, 2, 3$

Further

1

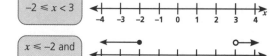

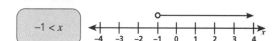

2 **a)** Tiff's inequality only includes down to −2. −2 is the smallest integer solution but non-integer solutions such as −2.99 and $-2\frac{2}{5}$ are possible.

 b) $-3 < x \leqslant 4$

3 **a)** $2x + 5 \leqslant 9$ and $3x - 7 \leqslant -1$

 b) $z = 16$

Pages 48–49
2.13 Non-linear sequences

Foundations

 a) $3n + 4$

 b) 304

 c) $3n + 4 = 60$ gives $n = 18.666…$, which is not an integer.

Fluency

1 **a)** 21 **b)** 10.5 **c)** 36

2 **a)** 3, 7, 13, 21, 31

 b) −1, 1, 5, 11, 19

 c) 0, 3, 8, 15, 24

3 **a)** 3rd term = $4a$

 b) 7th term = $29a$

 c) 10th term = $123a$

4 **a)** $2a + 3b + 3$, $2a + 6b + 3$, $4a + 9b + 6$

 b) $10a + 24b + 15$

5 $5 \times 2 \times 2 \times 2 \times 2 \times 2 \times 2 \times 2 = 640$

Further

1 **a)**

Position (n)	1	2	3	4	5
Term	12	18	18	12	0

 b) 6th term: $-3(6)(6 - 5) = -18$

 7th term: $-3(7)(7 - 2) = -42$

 sum: $-18 + (-42) = -60$

2 $\frac{1}{2}(11)(11 + 1) = \frac{1}{2} \times 11 \times 12 = 66$

3 **a)** $-2n + 3$, $4n - 1$, $5n$

 b) 6th term = $9n - 1$, 7th term = $14n - 1$

 $14 \times 5 - 1 = 69$

4 **a)** $4a$, $4ar^2$, $4ar^4$

 b) $4ar = 3$

 $4ar^3 = 27$

 $\frac{4ar^3}{4ar} = \frac{27}{3}$

 $r^2 = 9$

 $r = 3$, so $4a = 1$, so $a = \frac{1}{4}$

Pages 50–51
3F1 Working with ratios

Practice

1 **a)** 2 : 5 **b)** 25 : 3 **c)** 1 : 3 **d)** 5 : 2

2 3 : 4

3 $\frac{2}{11}$

4 Mario gets £120; Huda gets £180

5 £320

6 **a)** 48 kilometres **b)** 100 miles

7 48 cm

8 15 kilometres

9 **a)** 1 : 0.625 **b)** 1.6 : 1

10 $\frac{9}{20}$

Pages 52–53
3.1 Similar shapes

Foundations

a) 120 mm, 180 mm, 240 mm **b)** The angles are the same

Fluency

1 **a)** Scale factor is 3 **b)** $l = 15$ m

2 $73 \div 65 = 1.12307…$

 $139 \div 125 = 1.112$

 The scale factors are different so the notes are not mathematically similar.

3 TUS is an enlargement of XYZ by a scale factor 1.5

4 Scale factor = 2.5 **a)** 12.5 cm **b)** 3.2 cm

Further

1 Scale factor = $2\frac{2}{3}$

 $x = 10$ cm $y = 5.4$ cm

2 **a)** Scale factor = $75 \div 15 = 5$

 AB = 19 mm

 b) BC = 76 mm

3 The correct area scale factor is $3 \times 3 = 9$

Pages 54–55
3.2 Converting compound units

Foundations

a) 1000 **b)** 1000 **c)** 3600

Fluency

1 **a)** 0.4 km **b)** 0.0125 hours **c)** 32 km/h

2 $800 \div 167 = 4.8$ m/s

3 240 km/h = 240 000 m/h

 $240 000 \div 3600 = 66.7$ m/s

4 60 mph = 96 km/h, so yes he is driving within the speed limit **or**

 90 km/h = 56.25 mph, so yes he is driving within the speed limit

5 0.75 m = 0.00075 km and 5 seconds = $0.0013\dot{8}$ hours. In an hour, the tortoise travels 0.54 km and the hare travels 50 km. So the hare travels 49.46 km more.

6 $10.4 \times 60 \times 60 \div 1000 \div 1.6 = 23.4$ mph

7 75 cm² = 0.0075 m²

 Pressure = $\frac{300}{0.0075} = 40000$ N/m²

8 **a)** 45 m³ = 45 000 litres **b)** 112.5 minutes = 1.875 hours

9 Mass = density × volume

 $= 0.78 \times 2500 = 1950$ grams = 1.95 kg

 = 2 kg to the nearest kg

Further

1 18.4 grams = 0.0184 kg

0.95 cm³ = 0.000 000 95 m³

Density = $\frac{0.0184}{0.00000095}$ = 19 368.4 kg/m³

2 0.9 m³ = 900 000 cm³

7920 kg = 7 920 000 g

Density of bronze = $\frac{7920000}{900000}$ = 8.8 g/cm³, so silver has a greater density.

3 30 km = 18.75 miles

Time = $\frac{18.75}{12.5}$ = 1.5 hours = 90 minutes

The second person completed the race in 91 minutes and 13 seconds = 5473 seconds

30 km = 30 000 m

Speed = $\frac{30000}{5473}$ = 5.48 m/s

Pages 56–57
3.3 Direct and inverse proportion

Foundations

a) 30 minutes   **b)** decrease

Fluency

1 a) £22.40   **b)** 3.6 kg

2 a) 10 eggs   **b)** 75 cupcakes   **c)** 60 cupcakes

3 a) 100 days   **b)** 10 days

4 a) £24.50   **b)** 8 hours

5 a) i) 180 minutes   **ii)** 15 minutes

b) i) 36 minutes   **ii)** 22.5 minutes

6

g	6	2	5	4
h	5	15	6	7.5

Further

1 1 litre = £1.05 compared with 1 litre = £1.04

So no, they are not directly proportional.

2 a) 6 workers = 80 minutes so 5 workers = 96 minutes or 1 hour and 36 minutes

b) 80 ÷ 4 = 20 minutes, 6 × 4 = 24 workers

3 a) Direct proportion

b) Neither

c) Inverse proportion

4 In 1 hour, Bobbie would build $\frac{1}{3}$ of a wall. In 1 hour, Abdullah would build $\frac{1}{2}$ a wall.

$\frac{1}{3} + \frac{1}{2} = \frac{5}{6}$

So combined, in an hour they would build $\frac{5}{6}$ of a wall.

$1 \div \frac{5}{6} = \frac{6}{5}$ hours to build one wall

$\frac{6}{5} = 1\frac{1}{5}$ hours = 1 hour and 12 minutes

Pages 58–59
3.4 Rates of change

Foundations

1 a) €72   **b)** £50

2 3

Fluency

1 a) 12 litres/minute **b)** 360 litres **c)** 125 minutes

2 a) 8 bottles per minute   **b)** 80 640 bottles

3 a) £50   **b)** £10

4 a) Water is flowing out of tank A at a faster rate because the gradient is steeper.

b) The rate of change for tank A is 10 litres per minute. The rate of change for tank B is 4 litres per minute.

c) The rate of flow of the water

Further

1 a) Between 8 and 10 minutes because the gradient is greatest.

b) i) $\frac{200}{2}$ = 100 litres per minute

ii) $\frac{300}{6}$ = 50 litres per minute

iii) $\frac{300}{2}$ = 150 litres per minute

c) $\frac{800}{10}$ = 80 litres per minute

2 The water does not empty out at a constant rate as the gradient is not constant. Therefore, the rate of flow is not constant.

3 C – D (the rate of flow is constant)

B – F (the depth of water would increase at a faster rate at first, then it would slow down because the container is wider towards the top)

A – E (the depth of water would increase at a slow rate at first, then it would speed up as the container gets narrower)

Pages 60–61
3.5 Compound interest

Foundations

1 a) 1.35   **b)** 1.08   **c)** 0.85   **d)** 1.028

2 a) £5751.20   **b)** £18 400

Fluency

1 2000 × 1.03⁵

2 £14 196.73

3 393 cells

4 £57.80

5 Bank 1 will give £696.67 interest and bank 2 will give £504.68 interest. So bank 1 will give more interest.

6 5.6%

7 8 769 811 725

Further

1 9600 × 1.027⁸ = 11 880.50, so $n = 8$

2 4683.79 ÷ 3500 = 1.338 22…

$\sqrt[5]{1.33822...}$ = 1.06, so 6%

3 7000 × 1.04¹¹ > 9000 × 1.015¹¹, so after 11 years

4 1.1⁴ = 1.4641, so 46.41% increase

5 5120.22 ÷ 5186.78 = 1.013 so 1.3%

5120.22 ÷ 1.013⁵ = 4800

m = £4800 and x = 1.3%

Pages 62–63
4F1 Angles

Practice

1 $a = 138°$ $b = 323°$ $c = 40°$ $d = 50°$
$e = 45°$ $f = 45°$ $g = 41°$ $h = 111°$
$i = 75°$ $j = 105°$ $k = 94°$ $l = 50°$
$m = 81°$ $n = 35°$

2 50° and 80° or 65° and 65°

3 1080°

4 a) 10° **b)** 36

5 a) 45° **b)** 150° **c)** 105°

6 26°

Pages 64–65
4F2 Area and volume

Practice

1 a) 66 cm² **b)** 42 cm² **c)** 60 cm²
 d) 25π cm² or 78.5 cm² **e)** 26 cm²

2 12 cm

3 108 m³

4 8 cm

5 216 cm³

6 49 cm²

7 192π cm³

8 3.75 cm

9 24

10 140 cm³

Pages 66–67
4F3 Transformations

Practice

1

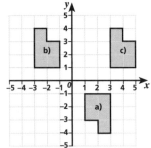

2

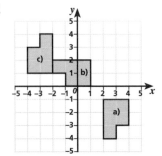

3

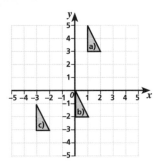

4

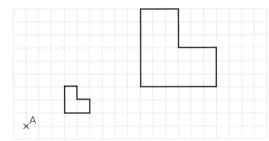

Pages 68–69
4.1 Constructions

Foundations

 a)–c) Check with a protractor.

Fluency

1 a) Check by measuring each side.
 b) Check by measuring each side.

2 Construction lines should be left.
 a) Each part should measure 22.5° (±2°)
 b) Each part should measure 52° (±2°)
 c) Each part should measure 120° (±2°)

3 Check by measuring. Original angle of 80° and each part 40°. Construction lines should be left in.

4 Check by measuring. Each part of the segment should measure 4 cm.

5 Check by measuring. Each part of the segment should measure 5 cm.

Further

1 Check by measuring angles (60°) and side lengths (7 cm). Construction lines should be left in.

2 Check by measuring lengths.

3 Line through A, at 90° to CD. Instructions below.

Place point of compasses on A and draw arcs intersecting CD; label these X and Y:

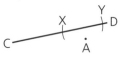

Then construct the perpendicular bisector of XY:

4 Line perpendicular to AB and going through P. Instructions below.

Place point of compasses on P and draw an arc

intersecting AB twice. Label these points X and Y:

Then construct the perpendicular bisector of XY:

5 First construct a 60° angle (as when drawing an equilateral triangle) and then construct its angle bisector.

Pages 70–71
4.2 Loci

Foundations

1–2 Check the accuracy of your constructions using a ruler and a protractor. See unit 4.1 for instructions.

Fluency

1 A circle, centred on O, with radius 5 cm.

2

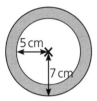

3 a)

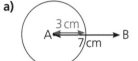

b)

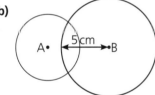

c)

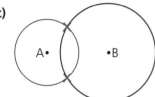

4

5

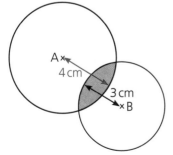

Further

1

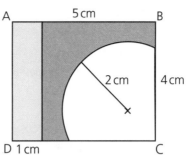

2

3

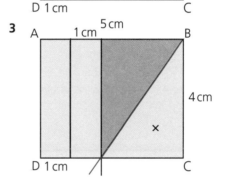

Pages 72–73
4.3 Parallel line angles

Foundations

  a) $a = 45°$ **b)** $b = 42°$ **c)** $c = 157°$

  d) $d = 97°$ **e)** $e = 40°$

Fluency

1 a) $a = 114°$ (alternate angles are equal)

  b) $b = 95°$ (corresponding angles are equal)

  c) $d = 100°$ (corresponding angles are equal)

    $e = 80°$ (angles on a straight line add up to 180°)

  d) $f = 42°$ (vertically opposite angles are equal)

    $g = 42°$ (corresponding angles are equal)

2 128°

3 $c = 121°$ (co-interior angles add up to 180°)

  $b = 59°$ (corresponding angles are equal)

  $a = 63°$ (angles in a triangle add up to 180°)

  $d = 122°$ (angles on a straight line add up to 180°)

  $e = 58°$ (co-interior angles add up to 180°)

4 Angle ADC = 118° (opposite angles in a parallelogram are equal)

  Angle EDC = 62° (angles on a straight line add up to 180°)

  Angle ECD = 56° (angles in a triangle add up to 180°)

5 Angle PQT = 49° (angles in a triangle add up to 180°)

  Angle x = 49° (alternate angles are equal)

Further

1 $2x + 30° = x + 70°$, so $x = 40°$

   $x + 70° + 2y = 180°$, so $y = 35°$

2 Angle FBC = 45° (angles on a straight line add up to 180°)

   Angle BCF (and BFC) = 67.5° (an isosceles triangle has two equal angles)

   Angle CFG = 67.5° (alternate angles are equal)

3 Angle OWX = 26°   Angle WXO = 35°   Angle WOX = 119°

4 No, because 79° + 105° = 184°. If parallel, they would be co-interior angles and should add up to 180°

Foundations

Rectangles measuring 2 cm by 3 cm and 8 cm by 12 cm

Fluency

1 a)

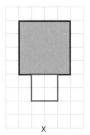

   b)

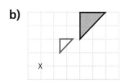

2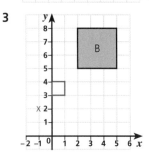

3
4 Enlargement, scale factor $\frac{1}{2}$, centre (5, 5)

Further

1 Enlargement, scale factor $\frac{1}{2}$, centre (4, 2)

2 a)

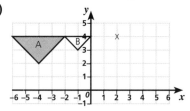

   b) Triangle A has area 4 units², triangle B has area 1 unit²

3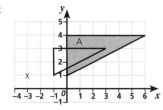

Foundations

   a) 42°   b) 123°   c) 75°   d) 98°   e) 273°

Fluency

1 a) 105°   b) 292°

2 a) 298°   b) 118°

3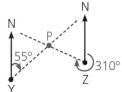

4 a)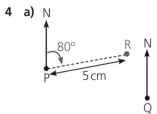

   b) 4.5 cm

   c) 346°

Further

1 a) 5 cm = 10 km

   b) 095°

   c)

   d) 6 cm = 12 km

2 340°

Pages 78–79
4.6 Parts of a circle

Foundations

    a) 95.03 cm²   **b)** 11π cm

Fluency

1 38.5 cm²

2 6π cm

3 5.0 cm

4 139 cm²

5 **a)** $\frac{56}{3}\pi$ cm²   **b)** 14.66 cm   **c)** 30.66 cm

6 **a)** 12 m²   **b)** 14.6 m

Further

1 **a)** $\pi r^2 = 90$, $r^2 = \frac{90}{\pi}$
    So $r = 5.35$ cm

    b) $\frac{1}{2}\pi d + d = 27.52$ cm

2 $6^2 - \pi \times 3^2 = 7.7$ cm²

3 **a)** Circumference $= \pi \times 24 = 24\pi$

    $x = \frac{4\pi}{24\pi} \times 360 = 60°$

    b) $\frac{60}{360} \times \pi \times 12^2 = 24\pi$ cm²

4 $\frac{\pi \times 6^2}{4} - \frac{\pi \times 3^2}{2} = \frac{9}{2}\pi$

Pages 80–81
4.7 Surface areas and volumes

Foundations

    a) 8 cm²   **b)** 21 m²   **c)** 64 mm²
    d) 160 cm²   **e)** 28.3 m²   **f)** 31.8 mm²

Fluency

1 **a)** $V = 140$ cm³   SA $= 166$ cm²
    b) $V = 198$ cm³   SA $= 234$ cm²

2 **a)** $V = 603.19$ cm³   SA $= 402.12$ cm²
    b) $V = 173.18$ cm³   SA $= 175.93$ cm²

3 **a)** $V = 100\pi$ units³   SA $= 90\pi$ units²
    b) $V = 288\pi$ units³   SA $= 144\pi$ units²
    c) $V = 66.666…$ cm³   SA $= 105$ cm²

Further

1 14 cm

2 360 cm³

3 $V = 135\,000$ cm³ $= 135$ litres
    $135 \div 3 = 45$ jugs

4 $294 \div 6 = 49$ (area of one face)
    $\sqrt{49} = 7$ (side length)
    $7^3 = 343$ cm³

5 Volume of cube $= 216$ cm³
    Solve $216 = \frac{4}{3}\pi r^3$ to get $r = 3.72$ cm

Pages 82–83
4.8 Congruent shapes

Foundations

    a) Isosceles   **b)** Isosceles   **c)** Scalene
    d) Isosceles   **e)** Equilateral

Fluency

1 **a)** D   **b)** F and B

2 **a)** 10 cm   **b)** 11.2 cm

3 B and C, using Angle, Angle, Side (AAS)

4 **a)** They are both right angled and have a side of 12 mm and a hypotenuse of 15 mm. So, they meet the RHS condition.

    b) All three sides are the same length in both triangles. So, they meet the SSS condition.

    c) They both have two sides the same length (14 m and 8 m) and the included angle in both is also the same (80°). So, they meet the SAS condition.

Further

1 Yes. If you work out the missing angle in the second triangle, it is 48°, so the AAS condition is met.

2 A and B – if you use Pythagoras' theorem in A (or B) you will see both triangles have sides of 3 cm, 4 cm and 5 cm. So, the SSS condition is met (or the RHS).

3 Example method:
    Side AB = side DC (because ABCD is a parallelogram)
    Side AD = side BC (because ABCD is a parallelogram)
    Both triangles have AC as the third side.

    So, both triangles have three sides of equal length, hence SSS condition is met.

Pages 84–85
4.9 Similar triangles

Foundations

    a) $6 \times 2 = 12$ **b)** $8 \times \frac{1}{2} = 4$
    c) $3 \times 3 = 9$ **d)** $4 \times 1.5 = 6$

Fluency

1 **a)** The angles in triangle MNP are the same size as the angles in triangle QRS, so the triangles are similar.

    b) MN $= 4.2$ cm

2 **a)** Scale factor is 1.5 $a = 27$, $b = 20$
    b) Scale factor is 2 $a = 10$, $b = 6$

3 **a)** Scale factor is 1.25 $x = 14.8$ cm, $y = 16.25$ cm
    b) Scale factor is 2 $x = 12.5$ cm, $y = 13$ cm

Further

1 Scale factor is $16 \div 12 = \frac{4}{3}$
    a) DE $= 8 \div \frac{4}{3} = 6$ cm
    b) AB $= 9 \times \frac{4}{3} = 12$ cm
    BD $= 12 - 9 = 3$ cm

2 Side ratios all the same: $\frac{10}{4} = \frac{7.5}{3} = \frac{5}{2} = 2.5$

3 Scale factor $= 2$ AX $= 7.5$ mm, BC $= 21$ mm

4 Side ratios all the same: $\frac{7}{2.8} = \frac{9}{3.6} = \frac{10}{4} = 2.5$

Pages 86–87
4.10 Pythagoras' theorem

Foundations

1 **a)** 16   **b)** 225   **c)** 42.25   **d)** 1.44
2 **a)** 5   **b)** 4.1   **c)** 6.5   **d)** 11.1

Fluency

1 **a)** 7.2 units   **b)** 4.1 units   **c)** 8.0 units

2 16.97 m

3 **a)** 15.9 cm   **b)** 95.4 cm²

4 **a)** 14.8 cm   **b)** 89.0 cm²

5 7.07 cm

Further

1 **a)** 11.18 cm   **b)** 11.87 cm

2 No. Maximum length is 13.27 cm (2 d.p.).

Pages 88–89
4.11 Trigonometry: missing sides

Foundations

a) $\angle$PRQ   **b)** $\angle$ABC   **c)** $\angle$LMN

Fluency

1 **a)** 5.9 cm   **b)** 6.5 cm   **c)** 11.0 mm

d) 0.9 cm   **e)** 21.8 cm   **f)** 9.4 m

2 CD = 13.6 cm, BD = 15.6 cm

3 5.8 m

Further

1 BD (by Pythagoras' theorem) = 11.3 cm

CD = 24.1 cm

2 **a)** BC = 20.4 mm   **b)** CD = 11.3 mm

3 AC = 20.12 m

AB = 20.12 − 8 = 12.12 m

Pages 90–91
4.12 Trigonometry: missing angles

Foundations

$\sin x = \dfrac{\text{opposite}}{\text{hypotenuse}}$ $\cos x = \dfrac{\text{adjacent}}{\text{hypotenuse}}$ $\tan x = \dfrac{\text{opposite}}{\text{adjacent}}$

Fluency

1 **a)** 35.7°   **b)** 60.6°   **c)** 41.4°   **d)** 41.8°

2 **a)** By Pythagoras' theorem, BD = 12.5 cm

b) 39.8°

3 **a)** BD = 5.35 cm   **b)** 24.0°

Further

1 $\tan$ ABC $= \dfrac{15}{9}$, so ABC = 59°

$x = 59 - 26 = 33°$

2 **a)** AE = 4 m (using Pythagoras' theorem)

b)

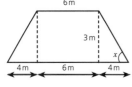

$x = 36.9°$

Pages 92–93
4.13 Exact trigonometric values

Foundations

a) $a = 60°$ **b)** $b = c = 45°$ **c)** $d = 30°$

Fluency

1 **a)** 30°   **b)** $\sqrt{3}$

c) **i)** $\dfrac{\sqrt{3}}{2}$ **ii)** $\dfrac{1}{2}$ **iii)** $\dfrac{1}{\sqrt{3}}$

iv) $\dfrac{1}{2}$ **v)** $\dfrac{\sqrt{3}}{2}$ **vi)** $\sqrt{3}$

2 1.5

3 60 mm

4 12 cm

Further

1 30°

2 4

3 $\sqrt{3}$

Pages 94–95
4.14 Vectors

Foundations

a) −24   **b)** −2   **c)** −2   **d)** 24

Fluency

1

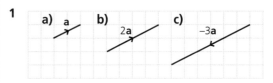

2 **a)** $\binom{3}{-1}$ **b)** $\binom{0}{-4}$ **c)** $\binom{-3}{2}$ **d)** $\binom{2}{0}$ **e)** $\binom{-3}{-3}$

3 **a)** $\binom{12}{-4}$ **b)** $\binom{8}{-8}$ **c)** $\binom{-7}{5}$

4 **a)**

b) $\binom{12}{-4}$

Further

1 **a)** $\binom{2}{7}$ **b)** $\binom{-2}{-7}$

2 **a)** $\binom{-1}{-4}$ **b)** $\binom{2}{8}$ **c)** $\binom{0.5}{2}$

3 Top row: $2(-4) - 3(b) = 7$, so $b = -5$

Bottom row: $2(a) - 3(2) = 0$, so $a = 3$

4 $3\mathbf{w} - \mathbf{x} = \binom{11}{-4}$

$\mathbf{y}$ is $2 \times (3\mathbf{w} - \mathbf{x})$, and this means that $\mathbf{y}$ and $(3\mathbf{w} - \mathbf{x})$ are parallel.

Pages 96–97
5F1 Probability

Practice

1 **a)** $\dfrac{1}{5}$ **b)** $\dfrac{1}{5}$ **c)** $\dfrac{2}{5}$ **d)** $\dfrac{3}{5}$ **e)** $\dfrac{3}{5}$

2 **a)**

+	1	2	3	4	5
1	2	3	4	5	6
2	3	4	5	6	7
3	4	5	6	7	8
4	5	6	7	8	9
5	6	7	8	9	10

b) **i)** $\dfrac{6}{25}$ **ii)** $\dfrac{6}{25}$ **iii)** $\dfrac{13}{25}$ **iv)** 0

3 1.4, −0.2 and $\frac{4}{3}$

4 **a)** 0.44 **b)** 112

5 $\frac{47}{50}$

6 0.45

7 $\frac{1}{6}$

Dice is fair, rolls are independent

8 **a)** Blue 0.2, Green 0.1 **b)** 50

9 **a)** 60

b) The probability stays the same and Amina does not improve/get worse.

10 a)

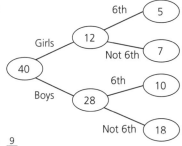

b) $\frac{9}{20}$

Pages 98–99
5F2 Statistical diagrams

Practice

1 37 − 32 = 5

2 **a)** $\frac{4}{27}$ **b)** $\frac{13}{27}$ **c)** $\frac{6}{27} = \frac{2}{9}$ **d)** $\frac{8}{27}$

3

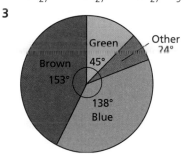

4

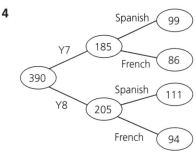

5 **a)** Negative correlation

b) Approx. £4000

Pages 100–101
5.1 Relative frequency

Foundations

1 $\frac{7}{20}$

2 480

Fluency

1 $\frac{125}{200} = 0.625$ $\qquad$ $\frac{15}{200} = 0.075$

2 **a)** 640 **b)** Red = $\frac{608}{1600} = 0.38$

3 **a)** $\frac{30}{120} = 0.25 = 25\%$ **b)** 0.3666...

c) The spinner seems biased towards green, but more trials are needed to be sure.

4 117

Further

1 **a)**

Total number of throws	10	20	30	40	50	60
Total number of goals	8	14	21	31	37	45
Relative frequency of scoring a goal	0.8	0.7	0.7	0.775	0.74	0.75

b)

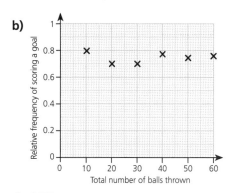

c) 0.75

2 Multiplying the relative frequencies by 20 and adjusting for total of 20 gives:

Green = 1 $\quad$ Red = 6 $\quad$ Blue = 9 $\quad$ Yellow = 4

3 **a)** $\frac{y}{x}$ **b)** $\frac{100y}{x}$

Pages 102–103
5.2 Combined events

Foundations

a) $\frac{1}{15}$ **b)** $\frac{8}{15}$ **c)** $\frac{7}{15}$ **d)** 0.06

Fluency

1 **a)** $\frac{1}{4}$ **b)** $\frac{25}{36}$ **c)** $\frac{1}{9}$

2 **a)** $\frac{2}{25}$ **b)** $\frac{12}{25}$

3 0.42

4 **a)** $\frac{1}{8}$ **b)** $\frac{7}{8}$

5 **a)** $\frac{1}{1000}$ **b)** $\frac{1}{100}$ **c)** $\frac{1}{8}$

Further

1 No. Both events have a probability of $\frac{1}{36}$

2 **a)** $\frac{5}{6} \times \frac{7}{8} = \frac{35}{48}$

b) $\frac{1}{6} \times \frac{1}{8} = \frac{1}{48}$

3 **a)** $\frac{7}{9} \times \frac{3}{7} = \frac{21}{63}$ (or $\frac{1}{3}$)

b) $\frac{7}{9} \times \frac{4}{7} + \frac{2}{9} \times \frac{3}{7} = \frac{34}{63}$

4 $\frac{5}{12} \times \frac{4}{11} = \frac{20}{132}$ or equivalent

Pages 104–105
5.3 Tree diagrams

Foundations

a) $\frac{8}{13}$ b) $\frac{15}{169}$ c) $\frac{6}{13}$

Fluency

1 a)

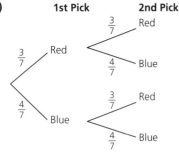

    1st Pick   **2nd Pick**

b) $\frac{9}{49}$

2 a)

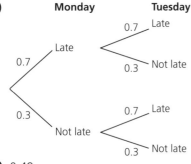

    Monday   **Tuesday**

b) 0.49

c) 0.51

3 a)

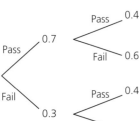

    Alex   **Mia**

b) i) 0.28 **ii)** 0.18 **iii)** 0.82

Further

1 a) $\frac{9}{169}$

b) $\frac{36}{169}$

c) $\frac{69}{169}$

2 a)

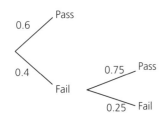

    1st   **2nd**
    Attempt   **Attempt**

b) 0.9

Pages 106–107
5.4 Sampling

Foundations

1 70

2 a) 520

  b) 581.54

Fluency

1 The number obtained when rolling a dice is random, hence the choice of the person with the corresponding number is also random.

2 a) The people who live in the town

  b) The 120 people asked

3 It only takes views of Year 11 students.
It is a small sample.

4 40%

Further

1 150

2 a) Running: 453; Cycling: 160; Rowing: 187

  b) More people who like running were there, so the sample is biased.

3 $\frac{180}{757} \times 50 = 11.88\ldots$, so 12

4 About $\frac{9}{80}$ of the population is 50
$\frac{50 \times 80}{9} = 444.444\ldots$, so about 450

Pages 108–109
5.5 Product rule

Foundations

1 60

2 12

Fluency

1 12

2 221

3 120

4 46872

5 190

6 4500

Further

1 $(10 \times 9) \div 2 = 45$

2 $209 \div 19 = 11$

3 a) 120 **b)** 20

4 a) $10 \times 10 \times 10 \times 10 = 10\,000$

  b) $10 \times 9 \times 8 \times 7 = 5040$

Pages 110–111
5.6 Cumulative frequency

Foundations

a) 40 b) 30 c) 45 d) 75

Fluency

1 a)

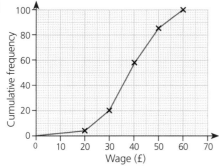

b) 40 (answers between 38 and 42)

2 a) Between 87 and 93 seconds

b) Between 15 and 25 seconds

Further

1 a) 29°C (answers between 27°C and 31°C)

b) 2 containers (answers from 1 to 3)

2 a) 100

b) 6

c) Yes. 10 travelled more than 15 miles. This is 10%

Pages 112–113
5.7 Box plots

Foundations

a) 17   **b)** 59   **c)** 14.5

Fluency

1

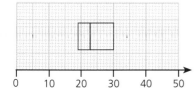

2 Fresh water fish have a higher median mass than salt water fish (they weigh more on average, 31 > 28). The masses of salt water fish are more consistent than the masses of the fresh water fish (smaller interquartile range, 10 < 17).

3 Comparing medians, school A had higher marks on average. Comparing interquartile ranges, school A's results were more consistent.

Further

1 a) 100   **b)** 150

2

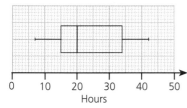

Pages 114–115
5.8 Averages from tables

Foundations

a) 80.2 g   **b)** 79 g   **c)** 72 g

Fluency

1 a) 2.3 cups (to 1 d.p.)   **b)** 2 cups   **c)** 3 cups

2 a) 11   **b)** 7300 steps

c) The data is grouped so we cannot be sure how many steps were taken by the people in each group.

Further

a) $5 < y \leqslant 15$

b) 13.45 m

c) The modal class interval would remain the same, but the mean height would increase.

Pages 116–117
5.9 Making inferences

Foundations

a) No correlation

b) Positive correlation

c) Negative correlation

d) Positive correlation

Fluency

1 The data Sana is estimating is outside of the given data.

2 a) Positive correlation

b) The number of butterflies in a garden will not have a direct effect on the number of people attending a water park. Correlation does not imply causation.

Further

a)

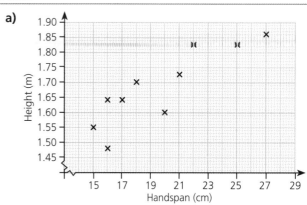

b) Positive correlation, **or**

The greater the handspan of a person, the greater their height.

c)

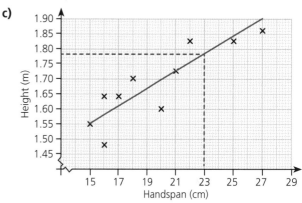

1.78 m (Accept answers in range 1.73 m to 1.83 m)

d) This data is outside of the given points on the scatter graph.

Index